C000195428

October 2007 – March 2008
OPG Annual Report and Accounts

Annual report by the Public Guardian to the Lord Chancellor on the discharge of his functions, presented to Parliament pursuant to Section 60 of the Mental Capacity Act.

Report and Accounts of the Office of the Public Guardian for the period October 2007 to March 2008, presented to Parliament pursuant to Section 7(2) of the Government Resource and Accounts Act 2000.

Ordered by the House of Commons to be printed 21 July 2008.

OPG 2007-2008

Our values

Accessible Making our services available to all who need them and providing an adaptable delivery of support, advice and choice.

Straightforward Conducting business in an open and honest way, respecting and protecting confidentiality.

Professional Treating our customers and staff with respect, working in partnership effectively and demonstrating personal and organisational excellence.

Progressive Being flexible and evolving by learning from experience to continually improve the service to our customers and the working environment for our staff.

People-orientated Fostering a learning environment to encourage our staff to develop and further their skills for the benefit of the business and to meet their personal goals.

Diverse Acknowledging the diverse society we serve and respecting and valuing this diversity in all we do.

How to contact us...

...By post
Office of the Public Guardian
Archway Tower
2 Junction Road
London N19 5SZ
Document exchange:
DX 141150 Archway 2

...Electronically
customerservices@publicguardian.gsi.gov.uk
www.publicguardian.gov.uk

...By phone
Customer literature and application forms:
0845 330 2900
(Mon-Fri 9am-6pm; calls charged at local rate)

General enquiries:
0845 330 2900

Text phone:
020 7664 7755
(Mon-Fri, 9am-5pm)

Fax:
020 7664 7705

Contents

Empowerment
Protection
Support
Choice

" Safeguarding rights and enabling and encouraging choice for all who need our services "

THE OPG VISION

Public Guardian's report

A review of his functions by the Public Guardian

As I prepare to depart from my role as Public Guardian, I present what is both my first and last Section 60 report. This new report specifically covers the statutory role and duties of the Public Guardian, and is separate from the annual report of the OPG as an agency. It is a requirement of the Mental Capacity Act 2005 (MCA) that this report is produced annually.

Since October 2007, I have been involved in the introduction of the MCA and the adoption of its principles throughout England and Wales. The Act breaks new ground and it potentially affects every citizen, providing empowerment, protection and choice to some of the most vulnerable people in society.

It has been pleasing to see the embedding of the new Independent Mental Capacity Advocates (IMCA) as part of the MCA. The IMCA service was launched in England in April 2007 by the Department of Health, and in Wales by the Welsh Assembly from October. It exists to help some of the most vulnerable people in society make important decisions about their lives, when there is no other close family or friend to help them decide. Health services and local authorities must consult the IMCA in these cases, and this new protocol is being increasingly acknowledged.

The encouragingly widespread use of the MCA has resulted in significant capacity issues for the OPG in its first six months and into 2008/09. The numbers making applications to the Court of Protection and to register Lasting Powers of Attorney (LPAs) have been far in excess of those predicted in the planning process prior to implementation. This has meant there have been considerable pressures on the OPG in coping with the workloads, including having to identify significant additional staff and the necessity of having to utilise large numbers of temporary staff to address the workload issues. This has also led to infrastructure issues, especially IT ones that are mentioned in the agency report. The agency, after initial difficulty, has begun successfully to expand its services to meet the requirements it set itself, although there remain delays in registering Powers of Attorney. For example, in June 2008, it was taking an average of 13 weeks against the agency target of a maximum of nine weeks to

The Public Guardian Board.

register LPAs that had no errors or omissions. The agency has a recovery plan that should lead to these operational difficulties being successfully dealt with in the near future.

The timescales involving the functions of the Public Guardian, such as the registration of LPAs and

issues around vulnerable people, although this has been made more complex to analyse by the initial delays customers have been facing. An important aspect of the forthcoming review of the Mental Capacity Act and the work of the OPG is to consider whether changes are required in this area and how they may be achieved.

Our recent independent customer survey of members of the public conducted in March 2008 showed positive customer feedback in most areas of the work of the OPG, with the customer satisfaction report highlighting a number of good performances. These included:

- The speed at which calls to the contact centre were answered;
- The clarity of the OPG information literature; and
- How well deputies were informed of, and understood, their duties.

However, these encouraging comments need to be considered alongside some individual comments in the survey, as well as the considerable concerns recently expressed by specialist solicitors working in this area who have yet to be surveyed. It is clear there is a need to engage with these concerns in the coming months.

There was considerable media and public interest in LPAs around the time of the introduction of the Act. Some groups raised significant concerns about the principles and approaches of the new applications process. These concerns were, in my view, inappropriate, and created an unduly negative perception of the

additional value they create for individuals.

In fact, based on our customer survey, individuals seem to be finding the process of completing the LPA registration forms – and the advice they receive from the OPG – acceptable, and, although it is significantly different from the process of registering Enduring Powers of Attorney (EPAs), it is not considered unduly complex. However, I have concerns regarding the process of registering LPAs – particularly where there are errors in a form. The legislation and related regulations mean the Public Guardian has very limited latitude in applications where there are minor omissions in completing the form. This means they have to be rejected by the Public Guardian, leaving that applicant with the choice of either an application to the Court of Protection for that LPA to be deemed valid, or re-commencing the process with an additional fee required. I have already looked at what can be done to address this by the Public Guardian and successful registration rates are increasing. However, the position remains that the EPA errors could be remedied by further amendments to the form, rather than having to resubmit it as in the case of an LPA.

I know my successor will continue to review how we can reduce the rate of rejection of registrations, and consider in the review whether anything further can be advised regarding process and regulations to ensure more LPAs are successfully registered.

those related to the Court of Protection, are primarily set out by legislation or regulation. A key factor in adopting the timescales was to provide greater protection to those involved in using the Act. It is becoming increasingly clear these timescales are often not what the customer expects or wishes to see when trying to deal with urgent

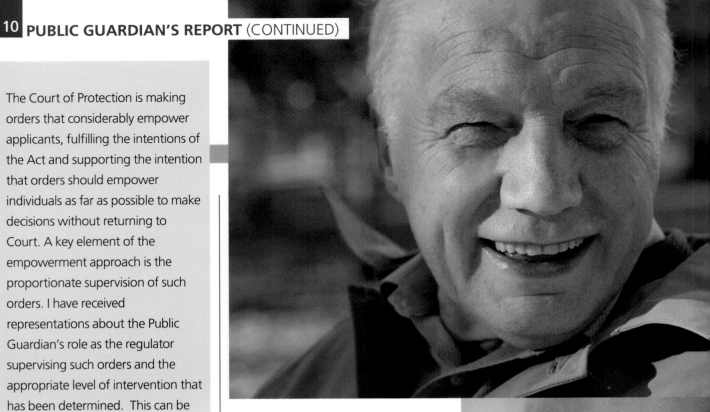

The Court of Protection is making orders that considerably empower applicants, fulfilling the intentions of the Act and supporting the intention that orders should empower individuals as far as possible to make decisions without returning to Court. A key element of the empowerment approach is the proportionate supervision of such orders. I have received representations about the Public Guardian's role as the regulator supervising such orders and the appropriate level of intervention that has been determined. This can be an area of some concern for individuals who dispute how closely the OPG can get involved in their case and scrutinise their actions. I believe we have developed a robust and fair system of regulation. However, the role of the Public Guardian in regulating Court-appointed deputies is a new one, and further changes may be required as the experience of this activity increases. Many individuals rightly receive a more proportionate approach in terms of supervision of their responsibilities under Court orders, involving less intervention where it is deemed appropriate. This has meant a greater focus on investigating and supporting situations where there are legitimate concerns or issues that need to be kept under review. In addition, the Public Guardian has been able to take a more active role in the regulation of Powers of Attorney following changes the MCA brought in. This has begun to lead to more active investigations of registered Powers of Attorney. The

Public Guardian was given no powers under the MCA to investigate or take action relating to the abuse of unregistered EPAs. This area remains one where I can only offer advice of alternative courses of action to individuals that approach the OPG regarding such situations.

As Public Guardian, I am required under regulations to charge fees for my services. The cost of registering an LPA is £150, rather than the previous EPA cost of £120. There is also a new fee regime for Court applications and the supervision regime. There is an open and transparent exemptions and remissions policy that is seeing positive up-take. While there have been some comments regarding the new fee structure, the main and understandable issue has been where the service has not been within the published timescales. Hopefully the recovery process that is underway will address this specific concern.

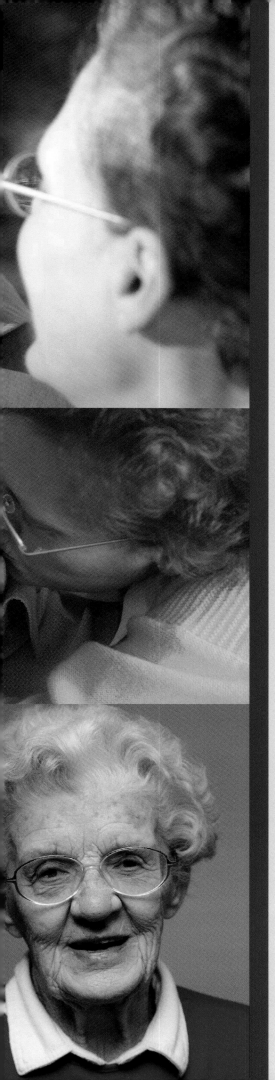

As there is a new statutory post of Public Guardian, there are new governance arrangements relating to the post. In my role as Public Guardian, I am required to exercise responsibilities relating to specific functions under the legislation. As head of an executive agency, I have accountability to Parliament as an accounting officer and to my sponsoring ministry (the MoJ). As a result, I am supported in my role as Public Guardian by an Agency Board, with non-executive directors, who advise me. In addition, the legislation requires that I am scrutinised in relation to the way I discharge my duties by a newly created Public Guardian Board, chaired by Rosie Varley OBE. The role of the seven independent Board members is to scrutinise and report annually on the way the Public Guardian discharges his or her role. Two of the Public Guardian Board members, including the chairperson, have been members since the inception of the Agency Board, with its specific role of advising on the operational decisions of the OPG. While each of these arrangements makes sense within its own parameters, the current arrangements make for a complex set of governance arrangements with some inherent conflicts for an activity that involves only around 400 staff. Personally, I would welcome a speedy review of these arrangements to see if they could be simplified without losing the important requirement of the necessary scrutiny of the Public Guardian's statutory role.

A review of both the Public Guardian's role and the work of the OPG is scheduled for autumn 2008, a year after the OPG was created. This will involve all our stakeholders and will help shape the strategic planning of my successor as Public Guardian and Chief Executive of the OPG.

Since February 2006, I have been responsible for the OPG and its predecessor, the Public Guardianship Office. I am proud of what has been achieved in introducing the MCA and of some of the successes of the OPG. Of course, I have been understandably concerned about the administrative delays in some of the areas of work of the Public Guardian. These are being addressed and I am sure my successor will ensure customers will enjoy the service we set out to provide. Some of the areas highlighted in this report are wider than operational matters and the pending review will allow these to be seriously considered in light of the first 12 months' operation of the MCA.

I wish my successor, Martin John, who takes over as Public Guardian on 11 July, every success.

Richard Brook
Public Guardian
8 July 2008

Annual Report and Accounts of the OPG

"The OPG exists to protect the rights of those who lack the mental capacity to make decisions for themselves"

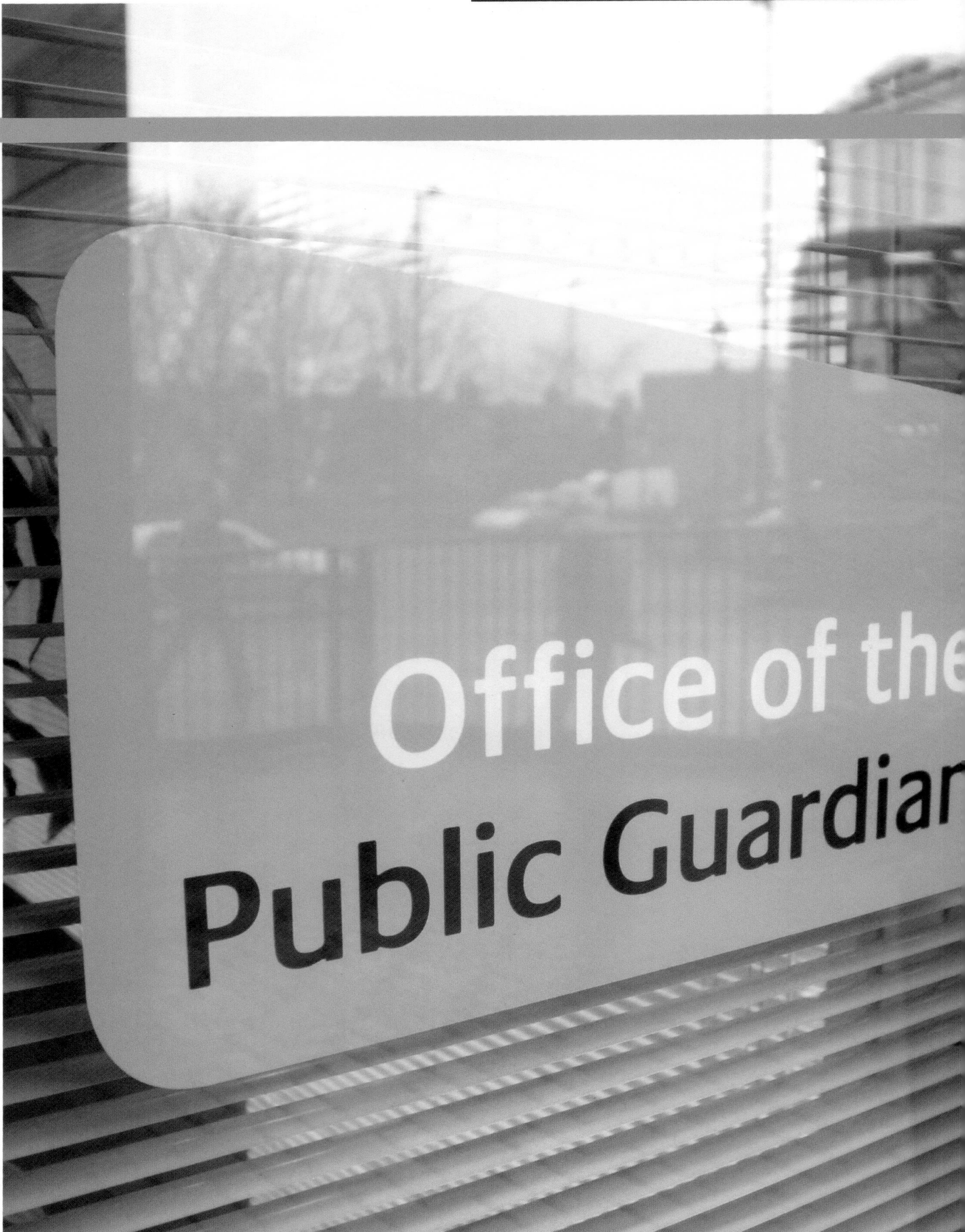
Office of the
Public Guardian

Welcome...

I am pleased to present the first annual report and accounts of the Office of the Public Guardian (OPG), for the period October 2007 to March 2008.

The OPG was created on 1 October 2007 with the implementation of the Mental Capacity Act (MCA). It replaced the Public Guardianship Office (PGO), which had been responsible for the protection of individuals' financial wellbeing since 2001.

The OPG has aimed to build on the success of the PGO, while at the same time taking on a much broader role as a result of changes brought in by the MCA. The Public Guardian has a much more robust regulatory role to play in safeguarding people's rights and has taken on the responsibility of supervising deputies. One of the biggest changes has been structural – the OPG and Court of Protection are now two separate entities, whereas previously the PGO was the administrative arm of the Court.

A clear line of integrity between the two bodies has been introduced. The OPG exists to protect the rights of those who lack the capacity to make decisions for themselves. Our role is to ensure that individuals – or those who represent them – are empowered to make decisions in their own best interests. We regulate and monitor the people who are appointed to manage the financial or health-related affairs of those who lack capacity. We also provide them with support and guidance, so they are aware of their responsibilities and are able to execute them effectively.

It is estimated that one in five people will experience some form of mental incapacity in their lifetime. Statistics show a growing number of younger people are affected by dementia. An increased awareness of mental illness, coupled with the far-reaching nature of the MCA, has meant that the work of the OPG has been much talked-about. Protecting one's welfare – both financial and health-related – in the event of incapacity to make decisions is a hot topic. More and more people are enquiring about what they should do to ensure their rights are respected and their needs are met, if the time comes when they are no longer able to make decisions for themselves.

Improving rights and awareness is undoubtedly a good thing, but the success of the Act and the publicity around its launch have generated enormous demand and placed the OPG under considerable pressure in some specific areas.

> **" It is estimated that one in five people will experience some form of mental incapacity in their lifetime – and statistics show a growing number of young people are affected by dementia "**

Workloads have been much higher than predicted in the MCA implementation business case. In some cases, we have seen an increase in volumes of around 200 per cent. In March 2008 we received 4,400 applications to register Enduring and Lasting Powers of Attorney (equivalent to 52,800 a year). By the time of writing, the monthly figure had increased to 6,000 (equivalent to 72,000 per year – nearly three times the number of applications received in previous years.) As a result, during the first few months of the OPG's existence that are covered in this report, we were not always able to meet customer expectations as effectively as we would have liked.

That has been a personal disappointment to me, and I want to apologise personally to those customers who have had a less than positive experience of the services in the first six months of the OPG's life.

Our staff have proved highly resourceful and resilient in reacting to the challenges presented by the changeover. It is a credit to them that the results of the first customer satisfaction survey carried out since the creation of the OPG were so promising, although I recognise some specific customer groups have expressed concerns regarding the services provided. As an organisation, the OPG is still

in its infancy, with plenty of areas to develop and improve, and considerable challenges ahead. It has successfully introduced new ways of working and has undertaken major change and, although it has had to cope with the unexpected and considerable demands on its services, its start has still been positive.

We are reducing the delays significantly and I believe once this has occurred the agency will be in a strong position to move ahead into the future.

I am not only required to report on the agency and present its accounts, I am required to report on the discharge of my statutory functions under Section 60 of the Mental Capacity Act. This report is on page 8 and it is there that I report on the workings of the Act and the experience since implementation.

Our performance – October 2007 to March 2008

Despite the challenges of establishing a completely new organisation, we have continued to strive for improved performance in the past six months. We set ourselves a robust and demanding set of key performance indicators (KPIs) and have worked hard to achieve those targets. In some instances, this has simply not been possible, as predicted workloads

were greatly exceeded. However, in many cases, even where there have been significant challenges, performance has been strong and recovery is underway.

During 2008/9, we aim to make our KPIs even more relevant, introducing more qualitative as well as quantitative measures. It is important that there should be a sense of shared responsibility across all departments and that KPIs 'cross-cut' the whole organisation, rather than remain within certain divisions. Crucially, we also need to start measuring our aims and their value, rather than simply the processes involved in achieving them.

Public Guardian Board

The Public Guardian Board was formally appointed in June 2007 – although it began working in shadow form in February 2007. The Board has seven members, including a member of the judiciary, and is chaired by Rosie Varley OBE. Between them, the members have experience and knowledge of areas covered by the MCA and the Public Guardian. The Board's duty is to scrutinise and review the way in which the Public Guardian discharges his functions and to make recommendations to the Lord Chancellor as appropriate.

In signing off, I would like to thank the non-executive directors of the OPG – Rosie Varley, Maurice Rumbold, and Bob Niven – for their work in providing advice and challenge to the activities of the organisation in its first six months. I would also like to thank the Audit Committee for their work with the OPG.

I am leaving the OPG for a new role outside the civil service, and would like to conclude by offering my sincere thanks to all the OPG staff and my senior management team. They have worked extremely hard in the face of considerable operational challenges.

Richard Brook
Chief Executive and Public Guardian
8 July 2008

> " The Public Guardian Board was set up on 1 October 2007 and has a very important scrutiny role. It is a significant safeguard for vulnerable people in that it's there to satisfy itself that the Public Guardian is operating effectively and in the interests of the public "
>
> ROSIE VARLEY OBE, CHAIR OF THE PUBLIC GUARDIAN BOARD

What is the OPG?

The OPG has replaced the Public Guardianship Office, and its new remit reflects the provisions outlined in the Mental Capacity Act (MCA).

The OPG is an executive agency of the Ministry of Justice (MoJ). It exists to safeguard the interests of people who may lack the mental capacity to make decisions for themselves, either now or in the future.

The Court is responsible for making decisions concerning the health, welfare and financial well-being of people who lack capacity, including the appointment of deputies (such as a relative, solicitor, or local authority).

The OPG supervises Court-appointed deputies, offering guidance and support in their decision-making, as well as overseeing their activity. The OPG is also responsible for the registration of Enduring and Lasting Powers of Attorney. The organisation employed 389 full-time equivalent staff as at 1 April 2008.

Ministers

The ministers with responsibility for the OPG are:

Rt Hon Jack Straw
Lord Chancellor and Secretary of State for Justice

Bridget Prentice MP
Parliamentary Under-Secretary of State at the Ministry of Justice

Our aims

■ **Protect rights**
We will work with others to ensure all those involved in the care of people who lack mental capacity understand their duty to act and make decisions only when necessary and only in the best interests of those for whom they are responsible.

■ **Support donors**
We will empower decision-makers, maintain records of powers granted and respond quickly and proportionately to allegations of misuse or abuse of power.

■ **Regulate and support deputies**
We will provide safeguards, assess and manage the risks and minimise bureaucracy and costs.

■ **Ensure high delivery standards**
We will monitor the delivery standards expected by our stakeholders and improve our service to reflect the expectations of a modern regulatory and administrative service.

■ **Develop policy**
We will lead on the development of Government policy on decision-making for people who lack mental capacity, emphasising the separation of judicial decision-making from regulation of deputies and attorneys, and policy development.

■ **Build partnerships**
As a new organisation, we will develop relationships with other relevant individuals, groups and organisations to ensure those who require our assistance are provided with a timely and appropriate service.

■ **Raise public awareness**
We will promote the MCA and provide information and advice to the public about mental capacity issues. We will highlight the choices available to enable people to make decisions on behalf of others who cannot do so due to lack of capacity.

Agency Board

The Agency Board as at 31 March 2008 consisted of six executive staff members and three external representatives (non-executives). Their roles are to develop the strategic direction of the agency. Each member has responsibility for overseeing a particular division and reports on the performance of that division to the Agency Board.

In addition, the Agency Board monitors the financial and business performance of the agency and identifies and manages risks. The Chief Executive of the agency, supported by senior staff, is responsible for operational activity, including the agency's commitment to equality in its activities.

The members of the Agency Board (excluding non-executive directors) during the financial year were all civil servants.

As at 31 March 2008, the Agency Board comprised:

Richard Brook
Chief Executive and Public Guardian

Louise Lawrence
Head of performance and change

Steve Rider
Head of customer contact centre

Craig McIlwrath
Head of applications and processing

Stephen Taylor
Head of finance and resources

Angela Johnson
Head of supervision

Rosie Varley
Non-executive director

Maurice Rumbold
Non-executive director

Bob Niven
Non-executive director

Financial activity

The agency is funded by the Ministry of Justice (MoJ), from its Parliamentary Supply and by income derived from fees and charges from external customers.

In common with other Government agencies, future funding has to be approved by our sponsor department the MoJ, and by Parliament.

Such approval has already been given for 2008/09 and there is no reason to believe that future funding will not be forthcoming. The financial statements have therefore been prepared on a going-concern basis for financial reporting and asset valuation purposes.

1 October 2007 to 31 March 2008
The OPG had a net cost of operations of £2.4m, which included £0.2m for the conclusion of the Mental Capacity Act implementation. The OPG's net assets at 31 March 2008 amounted to £10.7m, which includes the transfer of net assets from the former Public Guardianship Office.

Total operating income from fees relating to services provided to users of the Court of Protection and OPG was £9.2m. All fee-charging services must have a financial objective agreed with HM Treasury; details of the actual and target fee recovery are shown in note 6 to the financial statements.

The operating expenditure amounted to £11.3m, including staff costs for the Court of Protection and OPG of £6.1m, non-cash charges of £3.2m and non-staff operating costs of £2.0m.

> " The OPG Chief Executive, supported by senior staff, is responsible for the agency's operational activity "

An Act with impact

The Mental Capacity Act 2005 (MCA) came into force in October 2007.

The Act aims to empower and protect some of the most vulnerable people in society and to provide greater choice and flexibility in the ways their interests are cared for.

The OPG has played a key role in ensuring the effective implementation of the Act, which has the potential to impact positively upon the lives of almost every citizen in England and Wales.

The Act emphasises that everyone has the right to make their own decisions, and that they should be encouraged and supported to do so as much as possible.

If someone lacks the mental capacity to make a decision, they must be involved in the process of making any decision that affects them, such as those relating to their health, welfare or finances.

Importantly, a person's ability to make a decision should be assessed on a decision-specific basis. That is, just because they are unable to make one decision at one time, it shouldn't be assumed they can't make any decisions, or that they should be excluded from future decision-making.

Deputies (formerly known as receivers) and attorneys must follow the Code of Practice that supports the MCA when making decisions that affect the person whose affairs are entrusted to them. The Code of Practice provides practical guidance on how the Act works on a day-to-day basis.

The Act makes it possible for a person who currently has mental capacity to plan ahead for a time when they may need decisions to be made on their behalf.

On the ball to safeguard a client's best interests

Twenty-year-old Brian suffered a serious brain injury in a car accident. He is a big football fan and wants to buy a season ticket to see his local team play. His deputy, a solicitor, refuses to release the funds for the ticket. He feels it is impractical to do so, as Brian always needs to be accompanied to the games. Brian's mother contacts the OPG to ask for advice. The OPG feels the deputy's decision is unnecessarily restrictive and would have a negative impact on Brian's quality of life. The OPG contacts the solicitor and informs them that to act in Brian's best interests, they should release the money for two season tickets – one for Brian and one for his friend.

Five principles of the Act:

1 All adults have the right to make decisions for themselves, unless it can be shown that they are unable to make them.

2 Everyone should be given all the help and support they need to make a decision before anyone concludes they cannot make their own decision.

3 People are allowed to make what we might think is an unwise or eccentric decision – this doesn't mean they lack capacity to make a decision.

4 Any actions made on behalf of someone who lacks capacity must be done in their best interests.

5 People who lack capacity must not have their rights and freedoms restricted unnecessarily by the decisions made for them.

> **Around two million people in the UK lack the mental capacity to make their own decisions**

A new point of contact for customers

> **" It's great to feel that I've helped to resolve a query "**

CASE STUDY

Staff viewpoint:
Charlene Woolley
Customer service adviser

'I began my job in January, and it's been really interesting so far. We have a great variety of enquiries – from everyone from solicitors to lay people – about the changes that the OPG has gone through.

'A lot of what I do is educating people over the phone. It takes time for people to adjust, but the way we do things now is much easier. Occasionally we'll get a call from a client who has lost capacity, which can be difficult to deal with.

'The great thing is that my job is never boring! We're always talking to people and the atmosphere is very upbeat. We also discuss with each other the best advice to give in a certain situation.

'I find it so satisfying when I'm able to resolve a difficult complaint or query, especially if the caller is anxious. It's great to feel that I've helped them.'

The OPG's customer contact centre was set up in October 2007 to provide a central point of access for deputies appointed by the court, attorneys and others with general enquiries about the organisation and its work.

The contact centre deals with customer correspondence by phone, post and email.

It was originally anticipated that there would be around 700 phone calls each day, but in practice, the average number of calls received daily was well over 1,000. Call numbers were running at approximately 1,350 per day by March 2008. As a result of this unexpectedly high call volume, we directed resources towards responding to calls, rather than other correspondence. Each staff member handles up to 80 calls per day, and the total number of calls taken in the organisation's first six months was around 160,000.

To keep up with this challenging workload, extra resources have also been added. There are currently approximately 50 contact centre staff, of whom 30 are dedicated to phone lines. Around 45 per cent of staff are currently sourced from agencies and a permanent-staff recruitment drive is underway. Systems at the contact centre are professional, modern and efficient. Calls are recorded for training purposes, as well as being routed to the most appropriate team to deal with an enquiry.

Calls to the contact centre are diverse in nature. For example, a customer may require general advice on what they should do when a friend or relative loses capacity, or an existing deputy may call to clarify what s/he can do under the Mental Capacity Act (MCA).

LI=10 AV=1 CW=0 LW=00:00 AB=1%
PCA=88% VOL=108 10:14AM 23/04/08

Planned rates of response:

- **Calls:** 85 per cent answered within 60 seconds
- **Callbacks:** within 48 hours
- **Forms despatch:** within 48 hours
- **Letters:** within 15 days
- **Emails:** within 15 days

Staff training covers:

- Telephone manner and listening skills
- Technical elements of EPAs/LPAs
- Core applications
- Systems (process)
- Mentoring and feedback
- Reviewing and updating processes

> **Systems at the centre are professional, modern and efficient**

Other people may be looking for an update on the progress of their registration for a Lasting Power of Attorney (LPA), or some may require help because they don't understand the forms they are filling in. The centre is also the first point of contact for customer complaints, which have been relatively high as people adjust to the changes presented by the new Act.

Performance in the contact centre has been fair in the first six months. Our aim was to answer 85 per cent of calls within 60 seconds – in October 2007, we achieved this in 64 per cent of cases; by November, it was 75 per cent, and in March 2008 it reached the 85 per cent landmark.

More information is now being posted online and people are being encouraged to visit the website where appropriate to help manage the volume of calls.

Moving forward, the focus for 2008/09 will be to improve not just the rate of response, but also the quality. This will be measured through various means. Benchmarking, 'Mystery shoppers', post-contact interviews, surveys and other methods are all being considered.

The power
to protect

The introduction of the Mental Capacity Act and the launch of the OPG brought with them a change in the way people can apply for and register Powers of Attorney.

Before October 2007, people made (and later registered) Enduring Powers of Attorney (EPAs), which nominated someone to look after their financial affairs should they lack mental capacity in the future.

Once an EPA was made it could be used right away. When the donor lost capacity, the attorney was required to register the EPA as, until it was registered, the power could no longer validly be used (except for emergencies).

While no new EPAs can now be made, existing ones can be used and must still be registered when the donor loses capacity. EPAs have been replaced by Lasting Powers of Attorney (LPAs).

LPAs, although similar in principle to EPAs, have a number of key differences. In particular, LPAs can also be made to cover decisions relating to a person's health and welfare. For example, how and where a person would like to be treated should they fall seriously ill. There is a new comprehensive form for each type of LPA – and, unlike an EPA, an LPA can only be used after it is registered.

Because the Public Guardian now has a more active role in the notification process, the 42-day statutory waiting period for the registration of an LPA begins once the OPG sends out notice of receiving the LPA.

Publicity surrounding the introduction of LPAs had an impact on the OPG's work in the first six months. Also in the run-up to October 2007, media reports and legal advertisements encouraged people to make EPAs while they still could. As a result, there was a significant increase in EPA applications just prior to their replacement, and people who were using unregistered EPAs were also prompted to register them.

After an initial quiet period, the increased profile of LPAs resulted in a higher-than-anticipated influx of LPA applications when they came into force.

> " **The 42-day statutory waiting period for the registration of an LPA begins once the OPG sends out notice of receiving the LPA** "

Registering an LPA

Hassan is 55 years old and healthy. However, he has been thinking about his future and what would happen if at some point he became incapacitated. He has decided he would like to make provision for his daughters to look after his financial and health and welfare affairs should he lose capacity.

Having discussed his wishes with his daughters and those close to him, Hassan visits the OPG website and downloads the guidance booklets and LPA forms. He discusses what he wants to do with the people close to him, so they understand what his wishes are. Using the guidance provided, he fills in two application forms – one Property and Affairs LPA, and one Health and Welfare LPA.

Hassan makes a final check of the OPG website, looking at the most common mistakes made when filling out applications to ensure he hasn't made them. He also checks the guidance notes on fee exemption and realises he does not qualify. Satisfied his forms are completed in line with the guidance and have been certified, Hassan sends both forms to the OPG, along with cheques for the registration fees.

The OPG checks the forms and, finding they are filled in correctly, sends notifications to all the people Hassan has asked to be notified about the LPA registration. These people then have six weeks to make any objections to the registration.

No one objects to Hassan's applications so, after the six weeks, the OPG registers the LPAs and sends them back to him, stamped on every page. Hassan puts the registered LPAs away in a safe place and lets his daughters know where they are. They are now ready for use at any point in the future.

What are the key differences?

EPA Old system	LPA New system
Made prior to October 2007	Made after October 2007
Fewer safeguards against abuse	Greater safeguards under MCA
Finance	Finance or Health and Welfare
Valid before registration complete	Valid only after registration
35 days Statutory Waiting Period	42 days Statutory Waiting Period
SWP starts with date of customer letter	SWP starts with date of issue of OPG notices

The organisation had planned for an increase in registrations, estimating that there would be 30,000 applications per year – 20,000 EPAs and 10,000 LPAs. In fact, the current volumes are double that number, with LPAs forming the greater proportion (60 per cent) of the applications.

There were 2,697 new applications for LPAs in March 2008, with the vast majority relating to finance. So far, Health and Welfare LPAs have only formed around one-sixth of all LPA registrations. In March 2008 there were the same number of applications to register EPAs and twice as many applications to register LPAs, as there were applications to register EPAs in March 2007.

Because of this workload, the organisation struggled to cope with the demand. This meant that the rate at which applications were processed in the first six months was not as efficient as we would have hoped.

If there were problems with an application, or if the LPA form was incorrectly completed, it also took us longer than we wanted to return these to the person concerned, due to the high volumes.

The OPG is looking at ways to improve the service it provides. In particular, the aim is to acknowledge the receipt of an LPA more promptly, in order that the statutory waiting period can begin earlier.

It is our intention in 2008/09 to inform customers more quickly (within 10 days) when there is a mistake on their application.

Since January 2008, there have been steady improvements in the efficiency of the applications processing systems. To tackle the huge workload, more resources in terms of both staff and equipment have been procured. The applications team has grown, from 30 to 50 staff members between October 2007 and March 2008, with further increases already planned into the coming year.

LPA forms are available to download and print from the OPG website.

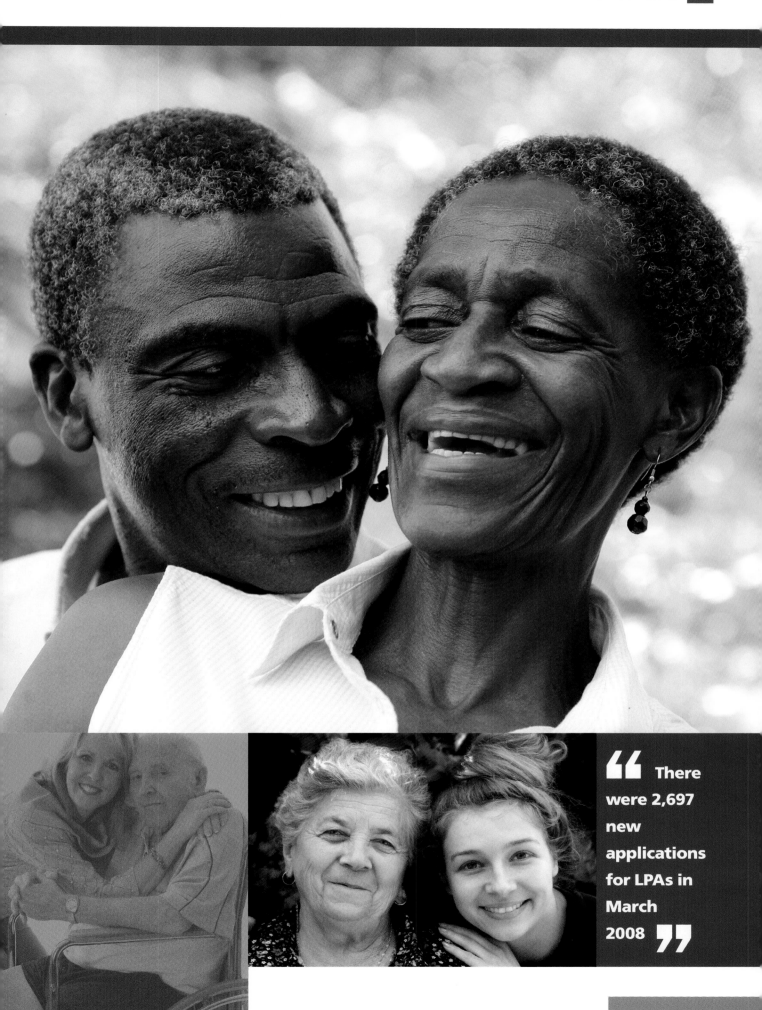

> " There were 2,697 new applications for LPAs in March 2008 "

Keeping a check on the deputy

The Supervision department became operational with the launch of the OPG in October 2007.

The department's function is to supervise the deputies appointed by the Court of Protection, making sure they're fulfilling their role and acting in the best interests of the person whose affairs they've been appointed to manage.

Most of the supervision we currently do is with regard to decisions about people's finances, although there are a small number of orders relating to people's welfare.

There are three levels of supervision that determine how closely a deputy is monitored:
I – Close
II – Light touch
III – Minimal

The criteria for deciding which supervision regime a deputy should be placed under are wide-ranging. For example, if a deputy has a poor credit history or concerns have been raised about their management of the funds, they are likely to be placed in the Type I category. If there are no concerns and the amount they are appointed to look after is less than £16,000, a deputy is likely to be placed in the Type III category.

However, there are also a number of other considerations that the supervision team take into account, such as the deputy's relationship with the person whose affairs they are managing, or how well they provide reports to the OPG.

Closely supervising a deputy may only be a short-term task for the OPG, to ensure particular requirements of the Court Order are met. A Type I supervision regime may be reduced after a period of time to a lighter touch, once the OPG is satisfied that the client's needs are being met.

Support and empowerment

Before the introduction of the Mental Capacity Act (MCA) and the launch of the OPG, permission needed to be sought before key decisions were made on behalf of someone lacking capacity.

Now, however, the focus is on empowering deputies to make decisions, involving the client wherever possible. Supervision is therefore crucial to ensure that deputies are not abusing their position. Since October the Public Guardian has had this regulatory role.

> **The closer the level of supervision, the higher the annual fee charged. This reflects the level of involvement and service received**

Protecting a client's interests

In the case of Miss Smith, 45, a visitor's report raises concerns about her living arrangements and the range of activities she is able to do during the day. There are also concerns about her vulnerability; there is a past history of financial abuse and, as she lives only with employed carers, there is a potential risk of this being repeated.

The OPG liaises with Miss Smith's deputy and her carers, highlighting the visitor's concerns. There has been some friction between the deputy and the carers in the past and we are able to address this by speaking to all parties independently. We also speake to Social Services to ensure they are involved in Miss Smith's case.

After several conversations with all parties, we arrange a further visit to confirm that the measures to improve Miss Smith's life have been put in place. The visitor's report shows there has been a great improvement.

The responsibility now lies with the deputy to justify the decisions that they make to spend money. For example, the OPG may want to know who the deputy consulted and how they reached a particular decision. It is more important that the deputy follows the Code of Practice and uses the funds in the client's best interests than that he or she accounts for every penny spent.

The OPG assesses each case on its own merit and looks in more detail at the major purchases made on behalf of the client – for example, where the deputy has made the decision to spend money having the client's property adapted for ease of use.

Supervision is not simply about regulating people or authorities who may be abusing their power. It's also about offering support to those struggling with the responsibility. It is important to recognise that Type I supervision could apply to someone who is undertaking their role as best they can, but needs help in places.

How does supervision work?
Each deputy assessed as needing close supervision is allocated a case worker, who produces a tailor-made case-management plan. The case worker is the point of contact for the deputy and keeps them informed of any developments, as well as talking to them to ensure that the client's needs are being met, and liaising with others with an interest in the client's welfare for their views on how the deputyship is working. The case worker will work with the deputy if action needs to be taken to improve things.

Case workers commission reports from visitors (see right) to ensure clients' needs are being met. They send as much information as they can about the case to the visitor, who then arranges a time to visit the client, and returns a report with recommendations to the OPG.

Where there is specific cause for concern, the OPG will investigate, as well this, we will also spot-check and audit 10 per cent of all cases subject to lighter-touch supervision each year.

If a deputy doesn't carry out their responsibilities correctly, the OPG will make an application to the Court to have them discharged from their role.

Investigations may result in an application to court to call in a bond, and where there are concerns over welfare or fraud, a case may be referred to Adult Protection Agencies or the police.

A visitor's role

There are 33 general visitors and 13 special (medically qualified) visitors based around the UK. Their job is to meet with clients at their homes to check that the deputy has made arrangements to meet their needs and that they are not open to financial or welfare abuse. Medically-qualified visitors can carry out assessments of a person's capacity to make decisions and provide reports to the Court.

Many of the visitors have a background in social care, health or probation, so they're very experienced at assessing whether a client's needs are being met.

At present, all the visitors are self-employed, but the OPG is planning to employ six visitors directly during 2008/09. This will give us greater flexibility and allow us to conduct a visit immediately if necessary. It will also give us more control over the training and development of visitors.

VISITOR

Visitor viewpoint:
Diana Gordon

'I work for the OPG as a visitor on a part-time basis. I have a background in health and social care and I've been visiting for three years. I see about 20 people a month and up to six or seven per day, spending an hour or so with each. When I'm there, I ask specific questions, such as "Does the deputy make contact with the client?" and "How are they making sure they fulfil their role?"

'Once I receive the commission from the OPG, I make an appointment a few weeks in advance. I've had two cases where there were serious concerns, so I had to respond to these more urgently.

> **" I've met some tremendous people and I love my job "**

'Sometimes a client is frustrated because their deputy isn't spending money on essential adaptations for the home. It can be complicated because often the deputy is a family member, but they're not acting in the client's best interests.

'I report back and advise accordingly, but out of the hundreds of cases I've had, there have only been a handful where there are genuine issues.

'I absolutely love my job. I get a lot of satisfaction and I've met some tremendous people who care for others in very difficult circumstances.'

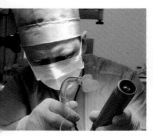

Before the introduction of the Mental Capacity Act (MCA), the key stakeholders that the agency needed to liaise with consisted mainly of those people who made applications, local authorities and solicitors' groups.

Now, because of the scope of the MCA, the groups and individuals that are affected by the work of the OPG are much more wide-ranging.

We need stakeholder involvement in order to evolve in line with the needs of people affected by the Act. When it comes to reviewing elements of the MCA or the way the OPG works, stakeholder feedback is very important to us, as we're not the people who are directly involved with caring for, or managing the affairs of, someone who lacks capacity.

The OPG has a strategy of proactive engagement with all our stakeholders. We aim to support stakeholders as much as we can and to communicate with them about key issues. We do this through a number of means, such as a quarterly newsletter, MCA Update, and other communications. We also co-ordinate two different consultation groups that each meet quarterly: The Court Users Group and The Stakeholders Group.

At these meetings we choose a number of key issues to discuss and consider ways of dealing proactively with these issues as well as listening to people's concerns.

The Public Guardianship Office had always had positive ongoing relationships with its stakeholders, and when the OPG was created, it was important to carry them on.

Supporting our stakeholders

Meet our groups

Court Users Group

This group is predominantly formed of solicitors and local authorities.

Stakeholders Group

The membership of this group is likely to evolve over time. We have deliberately invited as many people as possible that have shown an interest in the services provided by the OPG to be a part of the group, ensuring that a wide variety of service users are represented.

Our stakeholders include:

- Individuals
- Learning disability groups
- Primary Care Trusts
- Local authorities
- Doctors and nurses
- Nursing homes
- Adult protection officers
- Age Concern
- British Banking Association
- Solicitors

...and as awareness of the Act grows, the group of stakeholders keeps getting bigger.

Between October 2007 and March 2008, we provided four regional training sessions for local authorities involved in protecting the interests of people who lack capacity. There was a high demand for this information as the new provisions of the Act meant the work expected of local authorities was very different from the work they had been doing previously.

One challenge has been to gauge the level of involvement people expect from the OPG. We aim to manage our stakeholders' expectations as to what we do. It is important for us to understand the needs of different stakeholders, and for us to treat various groups appropriately, according to their needs. Operating pressures have meant that engaging with stakeholders has not been as robust as we would have liked. This is a priority for 2008/09.

The OPG is working on strategies to engage more actively with black and minority ethnic groups to communicate the requirements of the MCA. To this end, work has already been undertaken with both the Chinese Mental Health Association and the Afiya Trust, which represents African communities and other ethnic minorities.

What customers have said about **our service** so far

The first OPG customer satisfaction survey was carried out by MORI in March 2008. The survey asked different customers about a number of key areas and the results, a selection of which are set out here, are promising. The survey covered general members of the public; further surveys are due to be held with specific groups, such as professional advisers.

This research was completed by MORI, using a self-completion postal survey, conducted with five key customer groups. There were 2,229 responses (a response rate of about 40 per cent), which gives us confidence in these figures within seven per cent.

DEPUTIES

53% said they felt confident about the process of applying to become a deputy

CONTACT CENTRE

80% said the speed at which their call was answered was either very or quite good

83% said staff at the contact centre were either very or fairly helpful

SUPERVISION

71% of respondents felt the information they were given about supervision was very or fairly clear

87% of respondents said they understood why they had been allocated a particular level of supervision

COMMUNICATIONS

AROUND 70%
of people who had visited the website said they found it very or fairly helpful

AROUND HALF
of EPA/LPA respondents said they would prefer to be communicated with by letter, rather than newsletter

ENDURING/LASTING POWERS OF ATTORNEY

64% said it was very or fairly easy to complete the application form

73% said the information provided by the OPG was very or fairly helpful

94% said they understood their responsibilities as an attorney either very or fairly well

Communication tools we use

Website We began building the new OPG website in February 2007 and this went live in October. It's now much easier to navigate, forms and guidance are available to download

and there is now a search facility. Our aim is for the site to become a one-stop shop for media and public enquiries about the OPG.

Intranet A new intranet was launched following consultation with staff and an analysis of what people wanted. It contains essential tools to help staff do their jobs, as well as electronic versions of publications, such as the

staff newsletter *Update*, information about social events and links to useful web pages. It is also written in a more user-friendly language.

Newsletter (pictured far right) Since October, we have refreshed the OPG newsletter for deputies, which is now called *In touch*.

Events We attended a number of key events, including The Care Show and Learning Disability Today to highlight the work of the OPG. In addition, we also gave talks at a range of smaller, more local events.

Getting our message across

With the changes brought in by the Mental Capacity Act (MCA) in October 2007, there was a significant communications challenge for the OPG in the period before its launch.

Much of our external communications effort revolved around engaging and informing existing customers and stakeholders of the changes they should expect. We issued the customer newsletter *Reaching Out* and individual letters so customers were kept updated about the changes to come. We also regularly issued an electronic newsletter to stakeholders – *MCA Update* – and attended meetings with them.

A range of media guides, case studies and a DVD of three real life stories were produced to help raise awareness of the new legislation and the services it created, among the wider media. In particular, we targeted the specialist and trade press, such as *Nursing Times* and *Community Care*, and the financial sections of national papers, with articles about the changes that were about to occur. The communications campaign was successful and sparked a lot of positive interest.

Stories ran in national newspapers such as *The Times*, *Sunday Times*, *Daily Telegraph*, *Financial Times*, *Observer* and *Daily Mail* among others.

However, because of the huge media and public interest in the introduction of Lasting Powers of Attorney (LPAs), our communications strategy soon had to change tack. Rather than simply continuing on a proactive

OPG literature to advise and inform

We have produced guidance and forms to give people a clear picture of the work of the OPG and to explain what the Mental Capacity Act means on an everyday basis.

These materials are available to all, either through download from the website or in hardcopy from our customer contact centre.

As a matter of course, the vast majority of our materials are now translated into Welsh. The other languages in which OPG material is available are: Arabic; Bengali; Chinese; Gujarati; Hindu; Polish; Punjabi; Somali; and Urdu.

OPG information is available in an Easy-read format and we can also translate onto audio tape and into Braille, as well as providing DVDs using British Sign Language.

Our range of communication tools include a newsletter for deputies and a DVD.

information campaign, we needed to respond to a range of media reports, both positive and negative.

The unprecedented awareness of the changes coming into force led to increased workloads for frontline call-centre staff as well as those registering Enduring and Lasting Powers of Attorneys and LPAs. In an attempt to ease this situation, we initially adopted a targeted approach, in tandem with the

Ministry of Justice press office, to respond to media requests only where strictly necessary.

The Mental Capacity Act and its related services were formally launched by Bridget Prentice MP on 28 September 2007 at the Grange Day Centre for sufferers of Alzheimer's Disease. In addition, on 1 October, a range of stakeholders and staff took part in a launch event at Archway Tower.

> ❝ **The customer survey revealed a positive reaction to the new OPG brand and the way it has been communicated. People feel it is user-friendly and accessible** ❞

Valuing
our staff

The biggest impact of all the changes brought about by the introduction of the Mental Capacity Act (MCA) has been on the individual members of OPG staff who have needed to adapt not only to new roles within the organisation, but also to a whole new way of working under the Act.

Workloads over the past six months have been much higher than anticipated – in some cases resulting in a 200 per cent increase in volume. Teams that have been on the frontline have also had to help bring customers and clients on-board with the new structure and systems.

It is testament to their commitment and professionalism that staff across all levels of the organisation have adjusted so readily and reacted so positively to these challenges. Their support has been absolutely critical to the successful establishment of the OPG.

Staff development
The OPG is committed to developing and training its employees, so they are equipped with the appropriate skills and confidence to enable them to compete effectively for opportunities across the Ministry of Justice (MoJ) and other Government departments.

The emphasis on all learning and development – whether for managers or staff – is to ensure it is focused to meet the business needs of the organisation, as well as promoting core skills for a career within Government.

The OPG aims to build capacity and

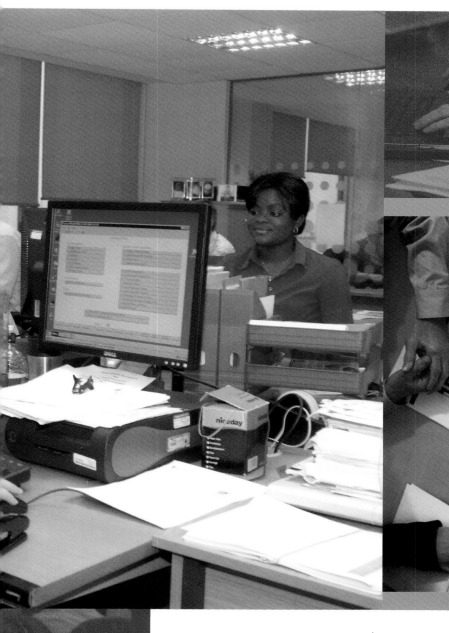

capability by ensuring vacancies are filled by the most appropriately skilled people, and that resources are used effectively.

Staff performance is monitored through mid-year and end-of-year appraisals and there are opportunities for staff to give feedback to their managers, through regular meetings.
Our aim is to create an environment where managers and staff have a two-way process of engagement. Employees should feel they can approach their managers, and managers should feel they can rely on their staff.

Supporting our staff
The OPG has a well-established work-life balance policy and operates flexible working patterns for staff, except where specific operational requirements mean this is not possible.

We aim to recognise and reward staff for exceptional service and do this regularly through 'Employee of the Month' and 'Team of the Quarter' schemes.

> " We're committed to training all our employees so they're equipped with the appropriate skills and confidence "

> **It is essential that staff are confident they will be treated fairly within the OPG** 〞

Any member of staff on a permanent or fixed-term contract is eligible to be included in the schemes, which aim to celebrate staff success in living out the OPG's values (see page 4) in their daily work. The process involves nominations being sought monthly (or quarterly) for any member of staff and an award panel – made up of two heads of department and two staff members – selecting a winner from these submissions.

The winner is presented with a trophy and letter to mark their achievements by the Chief Executive.

Support networks

It is essential that staff feel they can approach their managers and are confident they will be treated fairly within the OPG – whatever their background or beliefs.

There are a number of groups and networks within the OPG whose role is to support and provide useful information and advice to members.

These include:

Carers Network – for staff with caring responsibilities;

PROUD – for staff from black and minority ethnic backgrounds;

Rainbow – for gay, lesbian and transgender staff;

The Disability Network – for staff with disabilities; and

WIN – the women's issues network.

Sickness absence

Our target, in keeping with the Ministry of Justice (MoJ), is to reduce sickness absence figures to 7.5 days per person per year. While we have not met that figure, the overall number of sickness absences has gone down, from 10.04 during 2006/07 to an average of 9.82 per year in the period between October 2007 and March 2008.

Absences are managed locally within departments, and with due sensitivity to make sure we are doing everything we can to support people who are sick.

Managers have been given advice on how to manage sickness absence, through a workshop on good practice. The aim of this is to ensure that while each case is handled with flexibility, the policies for absence are applied consistently.

Staff retention

One challenge the OPG is currently overcoming is the retention of staff. Due to the changes, we had expected a relatively high

turnover of staff, and this has now reached 14.5 per cent.

Our human resources team is analysing the figures to identify the key staff retention issues, and then to plug the gaps systematically with a concerted and focused recruitment campaign.

We are also establishing a system of local exit interviews with leavers to find out whether there are particular trends in people's reasons for leaving.

As of March 2008, the OPG had around 25 per cent permanent vacancies across the organisation, most of which were filled by temporary agency staff.

Systems that support the business

The OPG is always striving to improve the way it works, and therefore we are committed to ensuring our computer systems are sufficiently flexible to allow us to do that. This includes updating and streamlining our computer systems so they are modern and effective.

At present, we have several systems, including CASREC and MERIS, for handling client data, which were updated as a consequence of the implementation of the Mental Capacity Act (MCA). Both CASREC and MERIS can be accessed by the contact centre to help them deal with customer enquiries.

We have created an IT sub-committee to help analyse how we can make IT work best for the

agency in the future. It is responsible for ensuring that all IT changes support the business functions and enable the capacity of the agency to grow.

During the first six months of the agency's life, the computer systems at the OPG were not as robust as we would have wanted them to be. In the coming year there will be an independent review of our IT systems and risks. The report from this will inform our planning. We will be working closely with the Ministry of Justice (MoJ) eDelivery group, who supply and oversee our computer systems, to ensure that we see improved service.

While there have been major improvements in our external IT offering, with crucial information and important documents now available on the OPG website, the application process for Powers of Attorney will continue to be paper-based. This is because Powers of Attorney currently require authentic signatures and real-time witnesses.

> **" We have created an IT sub-committee to help analyse how we can make IT work best for the agency "**

CASREC: The casework support system for cases where a deputy has been appointed. It holds: applications, which are recorded by the Court of Protection; information on clients and deputies; plus supervision levels and activities. CASREC currently stores electronic copies of all OPG outgoing correspondence.

MERIS: The casework support system for Enduring and Lasting Powers of Attorney. It holds information on applications, objections and registrations. It also holds electronic copies of incoming and outgoing correspondence.

Policies and priorities

Equal opportunities

The OPG is an equal opportunity employer. The aim is to be fair to everybody; to ensure that no eligible job applicant or employee receives less favourable treatment on the grounds of race, colour, nationality or ethnic or national origins, age, gender, sexual orientation, marital status, disability, religion or religious affiliation, or is disadvantaged by conditions or requirements which cannot be shown as justifiable. The OPG's policy builds on the Civil Service Code of Practice on Employment of Disabled People and the statutory obligations of employers under the Sex Discrimination Act 1975, the Race Relations Act 1976, the Disability Discrimination Act 1995, the Race Relations (Amendment) Act 2000, the Employment Equality (Sexual Orientation) Regulations 2003, the Employment Equality (Religion or Belief) Regulations 2003 and the Employment Equality (Age) Regulations 2006.

Learning and development

The Learning and Development department had two distinct priorities from the period just prior to October 2007 until the end of March 2008. The first was to work with the various areas of the agency to establish new processes and the second to devise and deliver, where required, appropriate training both on these processes and on the new IT systems supporting them. These varied from sessions suitable to cover the wide range of knowledge required by those employed in the new contact centre to the comparatively detailed single process requirements that are appropriate for the Supervision and Court teams. Having established the basic training protocols, these were then adapted and used to provide further training as staff were recruited or transferred into new areas of work.

Employee involvement

The OPG attaches considerable importance to ensuring the fullest involvement of employees in delivering its aims and objectives. It has therefore continued its practice of keeping employees informed on matters affecting them and on the performance of the agency. This is achieved through the OPG's intranet, a regular two-weekly newsletter, regular organisational briefings and circulation of press releases, annual reports and office notices. Formal and informal meetings are also held with employees, serving the purpose of consultation and feedback, as well as regular meetings with recognised trade unions.

> " The OPG's aim is to be fair to everybody; to ensure no eligible job applicant or employee is disadvantaged by requirement which cannot be shown as justifiable "

Creditor payment, policy and performance

The OPG pays all supplier invoices in accordance with the Government's payment performance targets. These require us to pay all invoices not in dispute within 30 days or within the agreed contractual terms. They also require us to pay 100 per cent of invoices, including disputed invoices once the dispute has been settled, on time within these terms. From 1 October 2007 to 31 March 2008 the OPG paid 98 per cent of invoices within this time span. Payments are only made once they have been properly authorised under the terms of the OPG's scheme of financial delegation. No interest was paid under the Late Payment of Commercial Debt (Interest) Act 1998.

Health and safety

The OPG recognises and accepts its legal responsibilities in relation to the health, safety and welfare of its employees, and of all people using its premises. The OPG complies with the Health and Safety at Work Act 1974 and all other legislation as appropriate.

In maintaining health and safety, a Health and Safety Committee meets quarterly to discuss relevant matters together with representation at the departmental Health and Safety Committee to keep informed of changes in legislation, practices, and procedures. Relevant training for staff and managers is provided to ensure compliance.

The OPG remains committed to continual improvement in this field, in consultation with staff and trade union representatives, who have played a constructive part throughout.

Sustainability

The OPG is committed to sustainable development, which can be defined as development that meets the needs of the present without compromising the ability of future generations to meet their own needs. The OPG implements the following strategies to support this statement.

Energy: Staff are reminded to switch off their CPU and monitor every night to reduce carbon emissions, while photocopiers and lights are switched off by security staff.

Resources: OPG booklets and forms have been printed on recycled paper, and the same content can also be obtained on a CD-Rom when requested. Clients are also encouraged to seek information via the internet and to email the office where possible.

Water filter machines are provided on each floor, which minimises the use of bottled mineral water and the need to operate individual kettles for hot water.

Recycling: Recycling points for paper, plastic bottles and cans can be found on each floor.

Transport: Staff members are encouraged to use public transport when travelling to an external meeting.

Report from the Court of Protection

"The Court's jurisdiction has been extended to cover health and welfare as well as finance"

Court's extended jurisdiction

The Court of Protection is a superior court of record, meaning it has the power to set legal precedents to be followed in future cases.

The President is Sir Mark Potter, President of the Family Division of the High Court, and the Vice President is Sir Andrew Morritt,

Vice Chancellor of the Chancery Division. Denzil Lush, former Master of the Court of Protection, is the Senior Judge and responsible for the day-to-day business of the Court. He is supported by four District Judges (three full-time and one part-time), all based at the Court's central registry at Archway, London.

There are also 43 District and Circuit judges throughout England

" Under the new Act, the jurisdiction of the Court of Protection was extended to cover health and personal welfare "

and Wales, including some sitting at the Principal Registry of the Family Division, who are nominated by the President to hear Court of Protection cases part-time at regional courts. In addition, certain serious matters must be heard in the High Court.

In preparation for 1 October, the Archway accommodation was reconfigured to include an additional court room, along with meeting rooms, a reception area and judges' chambers.

Under the new Mental Capacity Act (MCA), the jurisdiction of the Court of Protection was extended to cover health and personal welfare, as well as finance and property decision-making. The Court either makes the decision or appoints a deputy to make decisions on behalf of the person lacking capacity. However, the deputies must also have regard to the guidance set out in the Code of Practice, which supports the new legislation.

The judges also make orders in relation to registration of Enduring or Lasting Powers of Attorney. The increase in public awareness about the Act before its implementation resulted in an unprecedented increase in the volume of applications made to the Court from August onwards – and these

volumes have continued to exceed earlier predictions.

The regional courts designated in October as being appropriate for oral Court of Protection hearings were at Birmingham, Bristol, Cardiff, Manchester and Newcastle. Subsequently, a revised protocol provides for hearings to be held at the most suitable court. A total of 36 such regional hearings were held between October 2007 and March 2008, with a further 161 arranged at Archway.

As the Court continues to handle very high levels of work, not least because application volumes are still exceeding early predictions, it is looking to increase its judicial complement at Archway. This will ensure that timescales are reasonable, both for urgent or emergency applications, and for routine matters.

What is the Court of Protection?

The Court has the same powers, rights, privileges and authority in relation to mental capacity matters as the High Court.

It has the powers to:

■ Decide whether a person has capacity to make a particular decision for themselves;

■ Make declarations, decisions or orders on financial or welfare matters affecting people who lack capacity to make such decisions;

■ Appoint deputies to make decisions for people lacking capacity to make those decisions;

■ Decide whether a Lasting or Enduring Power of Attorney (LPA or EPA) is valid;

■ Remove deputies or attorneys who fail to carry out their duties; and

■ Hear cases concerning objections to register an LPA or EPA.

CASE STUDY

Transition scenario:
Making life more straightforward for Karen and her family

The Court in action

In these two scenarios the names and specific circumstances have been made up. But they illustrate typical examples of work carried out by the Court of Protection

Mr Carter was appointed receiver for his daughter Karen some years ago. This allows him to administer Karen's benefit and trust income, but gives him no direct access to Karen's capital, which is held in a high-interest deposit account at the Court Funds Office. To help him with Karen's care fees and general living expenses, Mr Carter arranged with the old Public Guardianship Office for a pre-arranged monthly sum to be paid into his receiver's bank account.

Under the terms of the Mental Capacity Act, Mr Carter automatically became a deputy in October 2007, although his powers remained generally the same. Mr Carter now wants to make some

improvements to the house Karen owns because she needs 24-hour carers.

As Mr Carter's current Order does not permit him access to Karen's capital, he makes an application under the existing Transition regulations for a lump sum to be released to him.

The officer refers the application and file to a District Judge so consideration can be given to providing Mr Carter with a deputyship order that will meet Karen's best interests, and to review the level of the security bond that may be required to cover any loss to Karen.

> " Mr Carter now wants to make some improvements to the house Karen owns because she needs 24-hour carers "

Health and welfare scenario:

Out-of-hours solutions for a complex case

> **The Judge initially makes an order that the NHS authorities cannot move Mary until various medical reports have been obtained and considered**

Mary is an 89-year-old woman who suffers from dementia and currently lives in an NHS hospital. She is due to be moved from the hospital into a nursing home, but her family does not think this is in Mary's best interests and is unhappy that the selected nursing home is some distance away.

Having exhausted the hospital's complaints procedure, the family members attend a review meeting late on a Friday afternoon. The NHS authorities are not prepared to reconsider their decision and have informed the family that Mary will be moved to the home on Monday morning.

The family consults a solicitor later that afternoon. The solicitor checks the Court of Protection section of the OPG website and also calls the OPG contact centre, out of hours. The solicitor is informed by the website and the out-of-hours recorded telephone message that for emergency applications made to the Court of Protection outside normal office hours, they must go directly to the Royal Courts of Justice.

Over the weekend, the solicitor acting for Mary's family makes an application to the designated Judge at the Royal Courts of Justice, who is sitting for urgent out-of-hours business. The Judge is authorised to hear Court of Protection business. The Judge initially makes an order that the NHS authorities cannot move Mary until various medical reports – and the report of an independent mental capacity advocate (IMCA) – have been obtained and considered.

The Judge further orders that, as Mary and all the parties are located around Birmingham, it will be more convenient for all parties if the matter is transferred and considered further by a suitable Court of Protection Judge at the Birmingham Court.

On Monday, the solicitor for Mary's family formally issues the application papers through the Court. The Court file is transferred to Birmingham where the matter will be decided at an oral hearing with all parties present.

OPG Finance and Accounts

"These accounts give a true and fair view of the agency's state of affairs at the year-end"

Remuneration report

Remuneration policy

The remuneration of senior civil servants is set by the Prime Minister following independent advice from the Review Body on senior salaries.

The salaries for the members of the Agency Board are determined by the Permanent Secretary of the Ministry of Justice (MoJ) in accordance with the rules set out in Chapter 7.1 Annex A of the Civil Service Management Code.

In reaching its recommendations, the Review Body has regard to the following considerations:
- The need to recruit, retain and motivate suitably able and qualified people to exercise their different responsibilities;
- Regional/local variations in labour markets and their effects on the recruitment and retention of staff;
- Government policies for improving public services, including the requirement on departments to meet the output targets for the delivery of departmental services;
- The funds available to departments as set out in the Government's departmental expenditure limits; and
- The Government's inflation target.

The Review Body takes account of the evidence it receives about wider economic considerations and the affordability of its recommendations.

Salary

'Salary' includes gross salary; performance pay or bonuses; overtime; reserved rights to London weighting or London allowances; recruitment and retention allowances; private office allowances and any other allowance to the extent that it is subject to UK taxation.

Benefits in kind

The monetary value of benefits in kind covers any benefits provided by the employer and treated by the HM Revenue and Customs as a taxable emolument.

Service contracts

Civil service appointments are made in accordance with the Civil Service Commissioners' Recruitment Code, which requires appointment to be on merit on the basis of fair and open competition, but also includes the circumstances when appointments may otherwise be made.

Unless otherwise stated below, the officials covered by this report hold appointments, which are open-ended until they reach the normal retiring age of 60. Early termination, other than for misconduct, would result in the individual receiving compensation as set out in the Civil Service Compensation Scheme.

Non-executive directors were appointed on a four-year fixed contract.

Salary and pension
entitlements

The following sections provide details of the remuneration and pension interests of the members of the Agency Board.

Remuneration

Members	2007-08 Salary £'000	Benefits in kind (to nearest £100)
Richard Brook Chief Executive and Public Guardian	55-60[1]	–
Louise Lawrence Head of performance and change	25-30[2]	–
Craig McIlwrath Head of applications and processing	25-30[3]	–
Stephen Taylor Head of finance and resources	30-35[4]	–
Steve Rider Head of customer contact centre	25-30[5]	–
Angela Johnson Head of supervision	25-30[6]	–
Rosie Varley Non-executive director	5-10[7]	–
Maurice Rumbold Non-executive director	0-5[8]	–
Bob Niven Non-executive director	0-5[9]	–

[1] Figure quoted is for the period 1 October 07 to 31 March 08. The full-year equivalent is £105k-£110k

[2] Figure quoted is for the period 1 October 07 to 31 March 08. The full-year equivalent is £55k-£60k

[3] Figure quoted is for the period 1 October 07 to 31 March 08. The full-year equivalent is £50k-£55k

[4] Figure quoted is for the period 1 October 07 to 31 March 08. The full-year equivalent is £60k-£65k

[5] Figure quoted is for the period 1 October 07 to 31 March 08. The full-year equivalent is £50k-£55k

[6] Figure quoted is for the period 1 October 07 to 31 March 08. The full-year equivalent is £50k-£55k

[7] Figure quoted is for the period 1 October 07 to 31 March 08. The full-year equivalent is £10k-£15k

[8] Figure quoted is for the period 1 October 07 to 31 March 08. The full-year equivalent is £5k-£10k

[9] Figure quoted is for the period 1 October 07 to 31 March 08. The full-year equivalent is £5k-£10k

Pension **benefits**

Members	Accrued pension at age 60 as at 31/3/08 and related lump sum £'000	Real increase in pension and related lump sum at age 60 £'000	CETV at 31/3/08 £'000	CETV at 31/3/07 £'000	Real increase in CETV £'000	Employer contribution to partnership pension account Nearest £100
Richard Brook *Chief Executive and Public Guardian*	0-5 plus lump sum of –	0-2.5 plus lump sum of –	58	27	24	–
Louise Lawrence *Head of performance and change*	10-5 plus lump sum of 40-45	0-2.5 plus lump sum of 0-2.5	218	178	10	–
Craig McIlwrath *Head of applications and processing*	10-15 plus lump sum of –	0-2.5 plus lump sum of –	182	146	7	–
Stephen Taylor *Head of finance and resources*	5-10 plus lump sum of 15-20	0-2.5 plus lump sum of 2.5-5	91	62	19	–
Steve Rider *Head of customer contact centre*	15-20 plus lump sum of 50-55	0-2.5 plus lump sum of 5-7.5	326	251	35	–
Angela Johnson *Head of supervision*	0-5 plus lump sum of –	0-2.5 plus lump sum of –	14	0	12	–

The opening balance of the CETV is stated at 31/3/07; the increase in CETV is for a full year.

Civil service pensions

Pension benefits are provided through the Civil Service Pension (CSP) arrangements. From 30 July 2007, scheme members may be in one of four defined benefit schemes: either a 'final salary' scheme (classic, premium or classic plus); or a 'whole career' scheme (nuvos). These statutory arrangements are unfunded with the cost of benefits being met by monies voted by Parliament each year. Pensions payable under classic, premium, classic plus, and nuvos are increased annually in line with changes in the Retail Price Index (RPI). Members joining from October 2002 may opt for either the appropriate defined benefit arrangement or a good-quality 'money purchase' stakeholder pension with a significant employer contribution (partnership pension account).

Employee contributions are set at the rate of 1.5 per cent of pensionable earnings for classic and 3.5 per cent for premium and classic plus. Benefits in classic accrue at the rate of 1/80th of pensionable salary for each year of service. In addition, a lump sum equivalent to three years' pension is payable on retirement. For premium, benefits accrue at the rate of 1/60th of final pensionable earnings for each year of service. Unlike classic, there is no automatic lump sum (but members may give up [commute] some of their pension to provide a lump sum). Classic plus is essentially a variation of premium, but with benefits in respect of service before 1 October 2002 calculated broadly in the same way as in classic.

The partnership pension account is a stakeholder pension arrangement. The employer makes a basic contribution of between 3 per cent and 12.5 per cent (depending on the age of the member) into a stakeholder pension product chosen by the employee from a selection of approved products. The employee does not have to contribute, but where they do make contributions the employer will match these up to a limit of 3 per cent of pensionable salary (in addition to the employer's basic contribution). Employers also contribute a further 0.8 per cent of pensionable salary to cover the cost of centrally-provided risk benefit cover (death in service and ill-health retirement).

The accrued pension quoted is the pension the member is entitled to receive when they reach 60, or immediately on ceasing to be an active member of the scheme if they are already aged 60 or over.

Further details about the CSP arrangements can be found at the website: www.civilservice-pensions.gov.uk

Cash Equivalent Transfer Values

A Cash Equivalent Transfer Value (CETV) is the actuarially assessed capitalised value of the pension scheme benefits accrued by a member at a particular point in time. The benefits valued are the member's accrued benefits and any contingent spouse's pension payable from the scheme. A CETV is a payment made by a pension scheme, or arrangement to secure pension benefits in another pension scheme, or arrangement when the member leaves a scheme and chooses to transfer the benefits accrued in their former scheme. The pension figures shown relate to the benefits that the individual has accrued as a consequence of their total membership of the pension scheme, not just their service in a senior capacity to which disclosure applies. The CETV figures, and from 1 April 2003 the other pension details, include the value of any pension benefit in another scheme or arrangement that the individual has transferred to the CSP arrangements, and for which the Cabinet Office's Civil Superannuation Vote has received a transfer payment commensurate to the additional pension liabilities being assumed. They also include any additional pension benefit accrued to the member as a result of their purchasing additional years of pension service in the scheme at their own cost. CETVs are calculated within the guidelines and framework prescribed by the Institute and Faculty of Actuaries.

Real increase in CETV

This reflects the increase in CETV effectively funded by the employer. It does not include the increase in accrued pension due to inflation, contributions paid by the employee (including the value of any benefits transferred from another pension scheme or arrangement) and uses common market valuation factors for the start and end of the period.

Richard Brook
Chief Executive and Public Guardian
8 July 2008

■ Further information about the work of the Civil Service Commissioners can be found at www.civilservicecommissioners.gov.uk

■ Further information about the work of the Review Body can be found at www.ome.uk.com

Corporate governance

Governance framework

The OPG Framework Document, laid before Parliament on 17 September 2007, sets out the financial and organisational framework within which the OPG operates as an agency and the responsibilities of those involved.

The Secretary of State for Justice and Lord Chancellor is the Minister accountable to Parliament for the activities and performance of the OPG. The Chief Executive is appointed to manage the OPG and the Secretary of State delegates to him or her responsibility for the exercise of its functions as set out in the Framework Document and for its day-to-day performance.

The Permanent Secretary for the Ministry of Justice (MoJ) is the Department's principal accounting officer and is the principal adviser to the Secretary of State on matters affecting the MoJ as a whole, including allocation of resources to the OPG, expenditure and finance. The Permanent Secretary, as principal accounting officer, must be satisfied that the OPG has adequate financial systems and procedures in place, both to promote the efficient and economical conduct of its business and to safeguard public and client funds.

The Permanent Secretary designated the Chief Executive as agency accounting officer for the Agency's administrative expenditure by letter, in a form approved by HM Treasury, which defined the Chief Executive's responsibilities and the relationship between the role of agency accounting officer and the role of principal accounting officer.

The Chief Executive

The Chief Executive is responsible for the management of the OPG. He or she is directly accountable to the Secretary of State for the effective, efficient and economic operation of the OPG. In particular, he or she is responsible for:

- Ensuring the proper management and propriety in handling public and client funds;
- Carrying out the functions entrusted to him or her by the courts or by statute;
- The quality of the service provided to clients;
- Setting operational policy and strategy;
- Managing the OPG's resources efficiently, effectively and economically;
- Risk management and corporate governance within the OPG;
- Preparing the OPG's corporate and business plans, and proposed key performance measures;
- Submitting quarterly performance reports to the Ministry of Justice;
- Achieving the OPG's agreed key targets;
- Preparing accounts and signing audited accounts;
- Operating an effective complaints procedure;
- Leadership of staff; and
- Ensuring effective consultation with the OPG's clients and stakeholder groups.

The Chief Executive, as agency accounting officer, is responsible for the proper and economical use of resources and expenditure of money voted by Parliament and for ensuring that correct procedures are followed for securing the propriety and regularity of public and client funds for which s/he is responsible. S/he is responsible for ensuring that the requirements of *Managing Public Money* as notified to him or her are met, and observes any general guidance on accounting matters issued to him or her by HM Treasury and the Cabinet Office.

The Chief Executive ensures that any recommendations of the Public Accounts Committee, other Parliamentary Select Committees or other Parliamentary Authority accepted by the Government and notified to him or her, are put into effect and provides regular reports to the Permanent Secretary on progress in compliance with such recommendations.

Relationships between the Chief Executive and the Court of Protection

The OPG as an executive agency of the MoJ is committed to delivering its priorities in partnership with the Court of Protection. The Agency provides administrative support for the Court and the members of the judiciary working for it.

The President, Vice President, and Senior Judge of the Court of Protection are nominated by the Lord Chief Justice of England and Wales, with the concurrence of the Lord Chancellor and Secretary of State for Justice.

The Senior Judge ensures the Court operates effectively, advises the president on interpretation of rules and regulations to ensure consistency of approach, and suggests practice directions where necessary.

The Chief Executive: provides support to the judiciary in carrying out its judicial and management functions; works closely with the judiciary in developing and implementing changes that directly affect the way in which the Court of Protection works; consults the judiciary on all other matters in which the judiciary has a legitimate interest; and only implements any changes after that consultation has taken place.

The Chief Executive and his or her staff work with the Court of Protection judiciary to ensure all parties are enabled to carry out their respective responsibilities.

In determining priorities across the OPG, the Chief Executive allocates available resources effectively. The OPG's annual priorities are discussed with the senior judge, as are plans for dealing with any major in-year change in resource allocation, which may materially affect the performance of the Court.

Judicial Service and Corporate Diversity Directorate (JSD), part of Access to Justice Business Group as of 1 May 2008, is responsible for the MoJ's overall policies in respect of judicial office holders, including their terms and conditions. JSD will lead on the annual liaison with the Senior Salaries Review Board in setting judicial salaries. JSD will provide services related to appointments (renewals, retirements) consulting with the OPG as necessary. The OPG will be responsible for the costs of the salaries and fees of the Court of Protection judiciary, and of their travel and subsistence, and will be consulted by JSD as appropriate.

Complaints

The Chief Executive is responsible for maintaining an open, fair and responsive complaints procedure in relation to the administrative work of OPG staff. The agency monitors all comments and complaints it receives and aims to respond constructively in line with the complaints procedure. Information on the OPG complaints procedure was published and made available to its clients on request and via the OPG website. It will be reviewed to ensure it is published in a manner that is clear and accessible to all users. An Independent Complaints Examiner (ICE) considers complaints that clients feel are not resolved after full investigation through the OPG's internal complaints procedure. The ICE reports regularly on its activities in relation to OPG complaints and, in the context of this work, provides considered advice to the OPG on improving customer service. Future reports will include detail on OPG relevant cases.

External auditor

The financial statements have been audited by the National Audit Office (NAO) on behalf of the Comptroller and Auditor General. No further audit services were received aside from that of Statutory Audit by the NAO. The cost of audit work was £45,000, which is solely related to audit services and is a notional cost (see note 5 of the financial statements). So far as the accounting officer is aware, there is no relevant audit information of which the OPG's auditors are unaware, and the accounting officer has taken all the steps that he ought to have taken to make himself aware of any relevant audit information and to establish that the OPG's auditors are aware of that information.

Internal audit

The Chief Executive, has established and maintains arrangements for the provision of internal audit services within the agency in accordance with the objectives and standards for internal audit set out in the Government Internal Audit Standards (published by HM Treasury) which include periodic peer reviews. The Ministry of Justice (MoJ) is provided with copies of the results of the peer reviews.

The MoJ Internal Assurance Division has a right of access to the OPG in support of the Permanent Secretary's responsibilities as principal accounting officer that includes access to all books, records, data, assets, personnel and premises of the OPG as may be considered desirable or necessary to discharge the department's responsibilities. The MoJ receives copies of the OPG's annual internal audit plans and annual report to the chief executive. The MoJ is notified of any fraud or irregularity within the definition set out in *Managing Public Money*.

Audit Committee

The OPG Audit Committee provides support to the accounting officer in the discharge of his responsibilities for governance, risk management, control and assurance. It is an advisory body and has no executive powers.

The members of the agency's Audit Committee during the period were:
- **Bob Niven**
  Chairman (Non-executive director)
- **Deep Sagar**
  (Non-executive director)
- **Kate Ivers**
  (Finance Division, MoJ)

The Chief Executive of the agency is an attendee. The Audit Committee met once during the period; internal and external auditors attended all meetings.

Deep Sagar is a member of the Public Guardian Board. No other Audit Committee member had any other directorship or significant interest that conflicted with their responsibilities as a member of the OPG Audit Committee.

Statement of accounting
officer's responsibilities

Under section 7(2) of the Government Resources and Accounts Act 2000 HM Treasury has directed the agency to prepare a statement of accounts for each financial year in the form and on the basis set out in their Accounts Direction.

The accounts are prepared on an accruals basis and must give a true and fair view of the agency's state of affairs at the year-end and of its income and expenditure, total recognised gains and losses and cash flows for the financial year.

The principal accounting officer for the Ministry of Justice (MoJ) has designated the Chief Executive of the OPG as the accounting officer for the agency, with responsibility for preparing the agency's accounts and for transmitting them to the Comptroller and Auditor General.

In preparing the accounts, the accounting officer is required to comply with the 2007/08 Government Financial Reporting Manual (FReM) issued by HM Treasury, and

in particular to:
- Observe the relevant accounting and disclosure requirements, and apply suitable accounting policies on a consistent basis;
- Make judgments and estimates on a reasonable basis;
- State whether applicable accounting standards, as set out in the FReM, have been followed, and disclose and explain any material departures in the accounts; and
- Prepare the accounts on a going-concern basis.

The responsibilities of an accounting officer, including responsibility for the propriety and regularity of the public finances for which an accounting officer is answerable, for keeping proper records and for safeguarding the agency's assets, are set out in the Accounting Officers' Memorandum issued by HM Treasury and published in *Managing Public Money*.

> **The accounting officer is required to comply with the Government Financial Reporting Manual**

Statement on internal control

Scope of responsibility

As the Office of the Public Guardian (OPG) accounting officer, I am responsible for maintaining a sound system of internal control that supports the achievement of the OPG's policies, aims and objectives; whilst safeguarding the public funds and agency assets for which I am personally responsible, in accordance with the responsibilities assigned to me by the accounting officer of the Ministry of Justice (MoJ) in accordance with the principles set out in *Managing Public Money*.

The OPG provides administrative resources for the Public Guardian and is an executive agency of the MoJ. The Secretary of State is the Minister accountable to Parliament for the activities and performance of the OPG. The agency has both an Executive Board and an Agency Board, which comprises the non-executive and executive members, who serve to provide strategic oversight, guidance, scrutiny of and challenge to the work of the OPG in support of the Chief Executive.

In addition, there is a Public Guardian Board (PGB), which has seven members independent of the OPG, including a judicial appointment made by the President of the Court of Protection. The Board's duty is set out in the Mental Capacity Act (MCA) and, in summary, it is to scrutinise and review the way in which the Public Guardian discharges his functions, and to make recommendations to the Lord Chancellor as it thinks appropriate.

The purpose of the system of internal control

The system of internal control is designed to manage risk to a reasonable level, rather than to eliminate all risk of failure to achieve policies, aims and objectives; it can therefore only provide reasonable and not absolute assurance of effectiveness. The system of internal control is based on an ongoing process designed to identify and prioritise risks to the achievement of the OPG's policies, aims and objectives, to evaluate the likelihood of those risks being realised and the impact should they be realised, and to manage them efficiently, effectively and economically. The system of internal control has been in place in the OPG from 1 October 2007 to financial year ended 31 March 2008 and up to the date of the Annual Report and Accounts, and accords with HM Treasury guidance.

Capacity to handle risk

I acknowledge my overall responsibility for the effective management of risk throughout my business area. I can confirm that registers to identify, assess and set out mitigating actions to significant risks are in place across my business area and are regularly reviewed at management boards. Risk management is incorporated into the planning and decision-making processes, with assessment of risk to business objectives documented, along with mitigating actions and reported on through risk registers and other means, which are (regularly) reviewed and updated:

- Risk is addressed monthly at the Executive Board meetings, and quarterly at OPG Agency Board and OPG Audit Committee meetings as an agenda item. Key risks are elevated to the MoJ Corporate Risk Register as appropriate;
- The OPG Corporate Risk Register is assessed and updated monthly by OPG Executive Board and reviewed by the Agency Board. The register includes details of risk, cause, effect and mitigating actions to manage risk with delivery dates, clear ownership and status of risk;
- Risk management is used in business plans – The Register details risks associated with achievement of objectives in the OPG Business Plan. Business performance is reviewed monthly by the OPG Executive Board and quarterly at the Agency Board;
- Project risks and status are reviewed by the OPG Performance and Change sub-committee as appropriate;
- A risk co-ordinator is responsible for maintenance of the Risk Register by calling for and collating updates from risk owners, liaising with MoJ Risk Management Branch, completing Statement of Assurance and Internal Control, and organising the Risk workshop; and
- The OPG provides information for the departmental fraud risk assessment.

The risk and control framework

There is a formal system for identifying, evaluating, managing and reporting risks to objectives, their impact, their likelihood of occurrence and current and planned mitigating action, along with assigned responsible risk owners:

- Use is made of the MoJ Risk Management Assessment Framework as a tool for the continued assessment of risk management in the OPG;
- The Risk Register and setting of top risks is reviewed monthly;
- The Risk Register is reviewed by the OPG Agency Board and OPG Audit Committee every quarter and by the OPG Executive Board monthly;
- A Risk Summary Matrix allowing risk to be prioritised and tracked throughout the period supplements the OPG Risk Register;
- The OPG Risk Register is provided to the MoJ quarterly to be considered in relation the Departmental Corporate Risk Register;
- Risk management is embedded in the activities of the business area including: policy making; project and programme; operational and performance management; business and delivery planning; and budgetary reviews;
- The OPG has a Security of Information policy and post-incident response plan;
- An information risk register and an information asset register are being developed;
- The OPG management control system has controls specifically covering security of information;
- The OPG staff recently received mandatory training in the security of information; and
- The OPG intranet, available to all staff, provides an Information Assurance and

Security section, which gives additional guidance on how to apply protective marking and a guide on how protective marking works.

Risk management is embedded in the activities of the business area, including: policy making; project and programme; operational and performance management; business and delivery planning; and budgetary reviews.

Public stakeholders are involved in the management of risks that impact on them. Key elements of this include:

- Partnership Forums exist for key groups of stakeholders, to maintain ongoing involvement of service users and stakeholder groups; and
- The OPG has an established and continuously updated and maintained Business Continuity Plan and Crisis Management Plans.

Other elements of an effective control system followed are: regular management information; financial and administrative procedures including segregation of duties; and a system of delegation and accountability.

Aspects of these other elements' arrangements are in place to ensure the following:

- Formal approval by the Agency Board of the business plans that are approved by the Minister and laid before Parliament;
- Comprehensive budgeting systems with an annual budget, which is reviewed and agreed by the OPG Executive Board and Agency Board;
- Delegated budget from the Department's principal accounting officer reviewed quarterly by the OPG Agency Board; and
- Sub-delegation to heads of department agreed and reviewed monthly at Executive Board meetings.

The OPG is not a stand-alone organisation and the maintenance of internal controls is reliant on the MoJ, which provides a number of key services to the agency including: Human Resources; Payroll; Information Technology; Facilities and Estates Management; Internal Audit; and Procurement.

The top risk priority for this period, which continues to be a prominent risk to focus on for 2008/09, is sustaining appropriate information technology to meet increasing demand for the services provided by the Court of Protection and the OPG.

Review of effectiveness

I also have responsibility for reviewing the

effectiveness of the system of internal control operating in my business area. My review is informed by the work of the executive and (senior) budget managers within the OPG and the Court of Protection, who have responsibility for the development and maintenance of the internal control framework, and comments made by the internal and external auditors in their management letters and other reports.

I confirm that I have carried out the review of the effectiveness of the system of internal control and an assessment of my key business risks, including the following key financial areas, and that all necessary controls are in place and have been applied.

All expenditure and income has been recorded and properly spent and received with regard to propriety and regularity:

- I have reviewed the stewardship reporting process in which Executive Board members, senior managers and team leaders have completed a statement confirming compliance with prescribed internal controls throughout the period, including the reporting of exceptions and remedial actions;
- I have reviewed the period report from the chairman of the Audit Committee; and

- I have reviewed the period report from the head of internal audit, which states that: 'It is internal audit's opinion that management can take a reasonable level of assurance from the arrangements established for governance, control and risk management in the newly formed OPG for the period ending 31 March 2008.'

There have been no instances of loss resulting from a weakness in internal financial control. Where such instances occur, these are reported and any necessary remedial action taken.

Significant internal control issues

There have been no significant internal control issues this financial year.

Summary

In this period I believe that we maintained reasonable levels of internal control, commensurate with the organisation starting its new journey.

Richard Brook
Chief Executive and Public Guardian
8 July 2008

Auditor's **report**

The certificate and report of the Comptroller and Auditor General to the House of Commons

I certify that I have audited the financial statements of The Office of the Public Guardian for the year ended 31 March 2008 under the Government Resources and Accounts Act 2000. These comprise the Income and Expenditure Account and Statement of Total Recognised Gains and Losses, the Balance Sheet, the Cash Flow Statement and the related notes. These financial statements have been prepared under the accounting policies set out within them. I have also audited the information in the Remuneration Report that is described in that report as having been audited.

Respective responsibilities of the agency, the Chief Executive and auditor

The agency and Chief Executive, as accounting officer, are responsible for preparing the Annual Report, which includes the Remuneration Report, and the financial statements in accordance with the Government Resources and Accounts Act 2000 and HM Treasury directions made thereunder and for ensuring the regularity of financial transactions. These responsibilities are set out in the Statement of Accounting Officer's Responsibilities.

My responsibility is to audit the financial statements and the part of the Remuneration Report to be audited in accordance with relevant legal and regulatory requirements, and with International Standards on Auditing (UK and Ireland).

I report to you my opinion as to whether the financial statements give a true and fair view and whether the financial statements and the part of the Remuneration Report to be audited have been properly prepared in accordance with HM Treasury directions issued under the Government Resources and Accounts Act 2000. I report to you whether, in my opinion, the information, which comprises the Financial Activity included in the Annual Report, is consistent with the financial statements. I also report whether in all material respects the expenditure and income have been applied to the purposes intended by Parliament and the financial transactions conform to the authorities which govern them.

In addition, I report to you if the agency has not kept proper accounting records, if I have not received all the information and explanations I require for my audit, or if information specified by HM Treasury regarding remuneration and other transactions is not disclosed.

I review whether the Statement on Internal

Control reflects the agency's compliance with HM Treasury's guidance, and I report if it does not. I am not required to consider whether this statement covers all risks and controls, or to form an opinion on the effectiveness of the agency's corporate governance procedures or its risk and control procedures.

I read the other information contained in the Annual Report and consider whether it is consistent with the audited financial statements. I consider the implications for my report if I become aware of any apparent misstatements or material inconsistencies with the financial statements. My responsibilities do not extend to any other information.

Basis of audit opinions

I conducted my audit in accordance with International Standards on Auditing (UK and Ireland) issued by the Auditing Practices Board. My audit includes examination, on a test basis, of evidence relevant to the amounts, disclosures and regularity of financial transactions included in the financial statements and the part of the Remuneration Report to be audited. It also includes an assessment of the significant estimates and judgments made by the agency and Chief Executive in the preparation of the financial statements, and of whether the accounting policies are most appropriate to the agency's circumstances, consistently applied and adequately disclosed.

I planned and performed my audit so as to obtain all the information and explanations which I considered necessary in order to provide me with sufficient evidence to give reasonable assurance that the financial statements and the part of the Remuneration Report to be audited are free from material misstatement, whether caused by fraud or error, and that in all material respects the expenditure and income have been applied to the purposes intended by Parliament and the financial transactions conform to the authorities which govern them. In forming my opinion I also evaluated the overall adequacy of the presentation of information in the financial statements and the part of the Remuneration Report to be audited.

Opinions

In my opinion:
- The financial statements give a true and fair view, in accordance with the Government Resources and Accounts Act 2000 and directions made thereunder by HM Treasury, of the state of the agency's affairs as at 31 March 2008, and of the deficit for the period, total recognised gains and losses and cash flows for the period then ended;
- The financial statements and the part of the Remuneration Report to be audited have been properly prepared in accordance with HM Treasury directions issued under the Government Resources and Accounts Act 2000; and
- Information, which comprises the Financial Activity included within the Annual Report, is consistent with the financial statements.

Opinion on regularity

In my opinion, in all material respects, the expenditure and income have been applied to the purposes intended by Parliament and the financial transactions conform to the authorities which govern them.

Report

I have no observations to make on these financial statements.

TJ Burr
Comptroller and Auditor General
National Audit Office
151 Buckingham Palace Road
Victoria
London
SW1W 9SS
15 July 2008

Financial

statements

Income and expenditure account
for the period ended 31 March 2008

	Notes	£'000	6 month period 2007/08 £'000
Income			
Operating income			
Fees income		9,230	
Fees remitted		(387)	
	2.1	8,843	
Other income	2.2	272	
Total income			9,115
Expenditure			
Staff costs	3.1	(6,071)	
Other operating costs	4	(2,064)	
Notional and other non-cash charges	5	(3,160)	
Total expenditure			(11,295)
Operating deficit before exceptional items			(2,180)
Exceptional items			(212)
			–
Deficit for the period			(2,392)

All income and expenditure are derived from continuing operations.

The notes on pages 70 to 83 form part of these accounts.

Statement of total recognised gains and losses
for the period ended 31 March 2008

	Notes	6 month period 2007/08 £'000
Deficit for the period		(2,392)
Gain on revaluation of tangible fixed assets	14	212
Total recognised losses for the period		(2,180)

Balance sheet
as at 31 March 2008

	Notes	31 March 2008 £'000	1 October 2007 £'000
Fixed assets			
Tangible fixed assets	8	4,946	5,214
Current assets			
Debtors	9	7,698	6,439
Cash at bank and in hand	10	563	405
		8,261	6,844
Creditors (amounts falling due within one year)	11	(1,408)	(1,317)
Net current assets		6,853	5,527
Total assets less current liabilities		11,799	10,741
Creditors (amounts falling due after more than one year)	11	(36)	(60)
Provisions for liabilities and charges	12	(1,058)	(1,073)
		(1,094)	(1,133)
Total net assets		10,705	9,608
Taxpayers' equity			
General fund	13	10,365	9,436
Revaluation reserve	14	340	172
		10,705	9,608

Richard Brook
Chief Executive and Public Guardian
8 July 2008

Cash flow statement
for the period ended 31 March 2008

	Notes	6 month period 2007/08 £'000
Net cash inflow (outflow) from operating activities	15	(214)
Capital expenditure and financial investment		
Tangible fixed assets additions	8/11	(561)
Financing		
MoJ funding	13	933
Increase in cash in the period	10	158

The notes on pages 70 to 83 form part of these accounts.

1 STATEMENT OF ACCOUNTING POLICIES

1.1 BASIS OF PREPARATION

These accounts have been prepared in accordance with the 2007/08 Financial Reporting Manual (FReM) issued by HM Treasury.

The accounting policies contained in the FReM follow UK generally accepted accounting practice for companies (UK GAAP) to the extent that it is meaningful and appropriate to the public sector. Where the FReM permits a choice of accounting policy, the accounting policy that has been judged to be the most appropriate to the particular circumstances of the agency for the purpose of giving a true and fair view, has been selected. The agency's accounting policies have been applied consistently in dealing with items considered material in relation to the accounts.

Without limiting the information given, the accounts meet the accounting and disclosure requirements of the Companies Act and the accounting standards issued or adopted by the Accounting Standards Board and HM Treasury, so far as those requirements are appropriate.

The agency is funded by the MoJ, from its Parliamentary Supply and by income derived from fees and charges from external customers. In common with other Government agencies, future funding has to be approved by our sponsor department, the MoJ and by Parliament.

Such approval has already been given for 2008/09. The financial statements have therefore been prepared on a going-concern basis for financial reporting and asset valuation purposes.

1.2 ACCOUNTING CONVENTION

These accounts have been prepared under the historical cost convention modified to account for the revaluation of tangible fixed assets at their value to the business by reference to their current costs.

1.3 INCOME RECOGNITION

Operating income is income that relates directly to the operating activities of the agency. It principally comprises fees and charges for services provided on a full-cost basis to external customers, net of fees remitted (see note 1.4) and net of VAT.

The Mental Capacity Act 2005 provides for fees to be charged in relation to proceedings brought before the by the Court of Protection; and in relation to the functions carried out by the Public Guardian. The levels of charges are contained in two statutory instruments. The Court of Protection Fees Order 2007 sets out the fees to be charged for matters coming to the new court and the Public Guardian (Fees, etc) Regulations 2007 sets out the fees to be charged for services provided by the Public Guardian.

Court of Protection fees
The Fees Order introduces a standard fee for all applications to court, which replaces all existing court application fees. The fee is payable upon making an application to court. It also introduces a new oral hearing fee, payable when the court makes a final order or decision at an oral hearing.

Public Guardian fees
The Regulations replace the range of fees that were payable by receivers appointed by the court with a single set-up fee, payable when a new deputyship is initially assessed for supervision; and a single annual administration fee. Cases are placed into one of three categories of supervision and pay annual fees according to the level allocated. The majority of cases fall into the Type II supervision category.

EPA and LPA registration fees
The registration fee is payable when the application is made.

A separate registration fee is payable for Property and Affairs LPAs and Personal Welfare LPAs when each application is made.

1.4 EXEMPTION AND REMISSION OF FEES

Both instruments provide for exemption and remission from fees. Exemptions apply to people in receipt of qualifying benefits who have not received a damages award in excess of £16,000, which has been disregarded for the purposes of eligibility for these benefits. The instruments also provide for fees to be waived or reduced, where, due the exceptional circumstances of the case, payment would cause undue hardship.

The Office of Public Guardian Finance Branch is responsible for authorising exemption from payment of fees and for approving applications to waive fees on exceptional grounds.

1.5 DEFERRED INCOME

Deferred income is that proportion of payments received which relates to services to be provided after the balance sheet date. Where the payment represents contributions to the funding of tangible fixed assets, the income will be realised to the Income and Expenditure account over the period of the underlying contracts determining these amounts.

1.6 PENSIONS

The provisions of the Principal Civil Service Pension Scheme (PCSPS), which is described in note 3.2 and the Remuneration Report, cover past and present employees. The defined benefit schemes are unfunded and non-contributory except in respect of dependants' benefits. The agency recognises the expected cost of these elements on a systematic and rational basis over the period during which it benefits from employees' services by payment to the PCSPS of amounts calculated on an accruing basis. Liability for payment of future benefits is a charge on the PCSPS. In respect of the defined contribution schemes, the agency recognises the contributions payable for the financial year.

1.7 CONSUMABLES

Consumables purchases (stationery and office supplies) are not considered material and are written off in the Income and Expenditure account as they are purchased.

1.8 LEASES

Where substantially all risks and rewards of ownership of a leased asset are borne by the agency, the asset is recorded as a tangible fixed asset and a debt is recorded to the lessor of the minimum lease payments, discounted by the interest rate implicit in the lease. The interest element of the finance lease payment is charged to the Income and Expenditure account over the period of the lease, at a constant rate in relation to the balance outstanding.

Other leases are regarded as operating leases and the rentals are charged to the Income and Expenditure account on a straight-line basis over the term of the lease.

1.9 NOTIONAL AND OTHER NON-CASH CHARGES

Notional and other non-cash charges are included in the Income and Expenditure account to reflect the full cost of the agency's services, in line with the FReM and HM Treasury's Fees and Charges Guide. These charges include:

Cost of capital charge
The cost of capital charge is a notional charge, which reflects the cost of capital utilised by the agency. The charge is calculated at the real rate set by HM Treasury (currently 3.5 per cent) on the average carrying amount of all assets less liabilities, except for amounts due to be surrendered to the Consolidated Fund (CFERs) and cash balances held at the Office of HM Paymaster General, where the charge is nil;

MoJ headquarters' support charges
The notional overhead charges for certain support functions provided by the MoJ; and

External auditor's remuneration
The notional charge for the statutory audit of the accounts carried out by the National Audit Office (NAO).

1.10 BAD DEBTS

Bad debts are written off when identified, or after a period of three years has elapsed from the date of becoming doubtful, whichever is the earlier. A general provision for doubtful debts is made based on the age of trade debtors as at the end of the financial year.

1.11 TANGIBLE FIXED ASSETS

Tangible fixed assets are stated at cost, including any costs such as installation directly attributable to bringing the asset into working condition. Expenditure on tangible fixed assets over £1,000 is capitalised. Where an item costs less than the prescribed limit, but forms an integral part of a package whose total value is greater than the capitalisation level, then the item is treated as a tangible fixed asset.

Tangible fixed assets have been restated using appropriate indices published by the Office for National Statistics (Business Monitor MM22). This is based on the modified historical cost accounting convention, which requires the revaluation of certain fixed assets in line with HM Treasury's FReM.

Revaluations above the depreciated historic cost of a tangible fixed asset are credited to a revaluation reserve. Amounts equivalent to the depreciation charge on the revaluation element are then credited to the Income and Expenditure account to offset the total depreciation charge on that tangible fixed asset, based on the revalued amount. Any downward revaluation of tangible fixed assets below the depreciated historic cost is charged directly to the Income and Expenditure account. Otherwise, it is offset against any balance in the revaluation reserve relating to that particular asset.

1.12 DEPRECIATION

Tangible fixed assets are depreciated at rates calculated to write them down to their estimated residual value on a straight-line basis over their estimated useful lives.

Assets under construction are not depreciated until the asset is brought into use or reverts to the agency respectively.

Estimated useful lives are as follows:
- Leasehold improvements — Remaining lease period.
- Furniture — 10 years.
- Equipment — 5 to 7 years.
- Computers — 5 to 7 years.

1.13 VALUE ADDED TAX (VAT)

The agency does not have an individual VAT registration with HM Revenue and Customs, but falls under the MoJ's registration, which advises the agency of any recoverable input VAT.

Irrecoverable VAT is charged to the relevant expenditure category or included in the capitalised purchase cost of tangible fixed assets. Where output VAT is charged or input VAT is recoverable, the amounts are stated net of VAT.

1.14 PROVISIONS

The agency provides for legal or constructive obligations, which are of uncertain timing or amount at the balance sheet date, on the basis of the best estimate of the expenditure required to settle the obligation. Where the effect of the time value of money is significant, the estimated risk-adjusted cash flows are discounted using the real rate set by HM Treasury (currently 2.2 per cent).

1.15 PRIOR YEAR COMPARATIVES

The OPG was created on 1 October 2007 under the Mental Capacity Act 2005 (MCA). The powers and responsibilities of the OPG are different from the predecessor bodies. Also, the organisational structure and fee regime are different. Therefore, it is not appropriate to include comparative figures.

2 INCOME

	6 month period 2007/08 £'000
2.1 OPERATING INCOME	
OPG fee income	(7,192)
remission	307
Net OPG fee income	(6,885)
Court of Protection fee income	(2,038)
remission	80
Net Court of Protection fee income	(1,958)
Net fee income	(8,843)

Fee income is shown net of fees remitted under the Public Guardian (Fees,etc) Regulations 2007 No. 2051 and the Court of Protection fees Order 2007 No. 1745 (L.13).

2.2 OTHER INCOME	
Charges for services provided:	
CAFCASS	(124)
CAFCASS deferred income	(24)
Recoveries in respect of outward secondments (see note 3.1)	(63)
Rental income	(61)
	(272)

3 STAFF NUMBERS AND COSTS

	OPG £'000	Court of Protection £'000	6 month period 2007/08 £'000
3.1 STAFF COSTS CONSIST OF:			
Salaries and wages	3,161	1,012	**4,173**
Social security costs	233	79	**312**
Superannuation	605	135	**740**
Agency/temporary staff	702	151	**853**
Contract staff	78	–	**78**
Total gross costs	4,779	1,377	6,156
Less MCA implementation costs	(85)	–	(85)
	4,694	**1,377**	**6,071**
Less recoveries in respect of outward secondments (see note 2.2)	(63)	–	(63)
Total net costs	4,631	1,377	6,008

3.2 The Principal Civil Service Pension Scheme (PCSPS) is an unfunded multi-employer defined benefit scheme. The OPG is unable to identify its share of the underlying assets and liabilities. The Scheme Actuary (Hewitt Bacon Woodrow) valued the scheme as at 31 March 2008. You can find details in the resource accounts of the Cabinet Office: Civil Superannuation (www.civilservice-pensions.gov.uk).

For 2007/08, employers' contributions of £740,261 were payable to the PCSPS at one of four rates in the range of 17.1 per cent to 25.5 per cent of pensionable pay, based on salary bands. The Scheme Actuary reviews employer contributions every four years following a full scheme valuation. From 2008/09, the salary bands will be revised but the rates will remain the same. The rates will be changing with effect from April 2009.

The contribution rates are set to meet the cost of the benefits accruing during 2007/08 to be paid when the member retires, and not the benefits paid during this period to existing pensioners.

3.3 The average number of whole-time equivalent staff employed (including senior management, judiciary, staff on inward secondments, agency/temporary staff and contract staff; but excluding staff on outward secondments) during the financial year was as follows:

By function:

	6 month period 2007/08 number
OPG	311
Court	76
Judiciary	5
Total	392

Total staff (including outward secondments):

	6 month period 2007/08 number
Civil servants	303
Agency/temporary staff	81
Contract staff	3
Judiciary	5
Civil servants on outward secondments to Liberata UK Ltd	3
Total	395

Staff costs (see note 3.1) for the Court of Protection include the administrative and judicial costs. Judicial costs are as follows:

	6 month period 2007/08 £'000
Salaries and wages	223
Social security costs	25
	248

4 OTHER OPERATING COSTS

	6 month period 2007/08 £'000
Cash losses and ex-gratia payments	19
Consumables	292
Maintenance	378
Travel and subsistence	13
Other running costs	266
Postage	133
Rates	151
Rental of accommodation	457
Utilities	133
Visitor services	222
	2,064

Other operating costs exclude £127,000 incurred as Mental Capacity Act (MCA) implementation costs and disclosed as exceptional items in the Income and Expenditure account.

5 NOTIONAL AND OTHER NON-CASH CHARGES

	6 month period 2007/08 £'000
Bad debts	10
Cost of capital charge	123
MoJ headquarters' support charges:	
E-delivery group	1,300
Facilities management group	382
Human resources division	182
Other	312
Depreciation	795
Loss on disposal of fixed assets	1
External auditor's remuneration	45
Provision for liabilities:	
Provided in the year	10
	3,160

There is no external auditor's remuneration for non-audit work.

6 FEES AND CHARGES

The agency is required, in accordance with *Managing Public Money*, to disclose results for the areas of its activities undertaken throughout the financial year, where fees and charges were made.

Ministers and HM Treasury agreed a fees strategy for the Court of Protection and OPG involving 63 per cent cost recovery for the Court of Protection and 100 per cent cost recovery for the OPG. This strategy was reflected in both statutory instruments and was implemented from 1 October 2007.

A subsidy is provided as planned to ensure clients are not denied access to services through the inability to afford the requisite fees. The calculation of cost recovery includes expenditure for claims and losses charged to the Income and Expenditure account.

(By business segment)	Court £'000	OPG £'000	Total £'000
Operating income	1,958	6,885	8,843
Fees remitted	80	307	387
Total income	2,038	7,192	9,230
Total expenditure	3,238	7,184	10,422
(Deficit)/surplus	(1,200)	8	(1,192)
Cost recovery (%)	63%	100%	89%

Reconciliation	£'000
Fees and charges (deficit)	(1,192)
Fees remitted	(387)
In-year bad debts	(10)
Mental Capacity Act costs	(212)
MCA transition costs[1]	(591)
Reported Income and Expenditure account (deficit)	**(2,392)**

[1]Staff costs migrating receivership cases to deputyship cases through the Court of Protection.

7 ANALYSIS BY ADMINISTRATION AND PROGRAMME

For public expenditure control purposes, the income and expenditure of the agency is classified between administration and programme. While this classification is reflected in the Operating Cost Statement of the Resource Accounts prepared by the MoJ, the agency considers it to be inappropriate for its executive agency accounts. For this reason the agency has taken advantage of the dispensation offered by the FReM for supply financed agencies, which are not whole departments, to adopt a Companies Act format for their Income and Expenditure account.

If the FReM format for an Operating Cost Statement had been adopted, the analysis of the deficit for the year would have been as follows:

Programme costs	6 month period 2007/08 £'000
Staff costs	6,071
Other operating costs	2,064
Notional charges	3,160
	11,295
Mental Capacity Act costs	212
Gross programme costs	11,507
Operating income	(9,115)
Net programme costs	2,392
Deficit for the year	**2,392**

OPG income and expenditure is classified as 100 per cent Programme based on an assessment of the work carried out by the OPG, which is mainly a frontline service; this classification has been agreed with HM treasury.

8 TANGIBLE FIXED ASSETS

	Leasehold improvements	Furniture	Equipment	Computers	Assets under construction	Total
	£'000	£'000	£'000	£'000	£'000	£'000
Cost or valuation						
At 1 October 2007	4,607	752	459	1,669	2,722	10,209
Additions/(reclassifications)	–	44	118	2,560	(2,406)	316
Disposals	–	(2)	–	–	–	(2)
Revaluation	183	4	121	36	–	344
At 31 March 2008	**4,790**	**798**	**698**	**4,265**	**316**	10,867
Depreciation						
At 1 October 2007	3,255	591	434	715	–	4,995
Provided in year	341	22	58	374	–	795
Disposals	–	(1)	–	–	–	(1)
Revaluation	129	2	1	–	–	132
At 31 March 2008	**3,725**	**614**	**493**	**1,089**	**–**	5,921
Net book value						
At 31 March 2008	**1,065**	**184**	**205**	**3,176**	**316**	4,946
At 1 October 2007	1,352	161	25	954	2,722	5,214

Leasehold improvements represents the refurbishment of the agency's headquarters at Archway. The Archway Tower Relocation Project was completed on 1 April 2002 and depreciation is being charged on leasehold improvements from this date over the remaining lease term.

Equipment revaluation includes £119,000 to reflect the re-lifing of the telephone system.

9 DEBTORS

	31 March 2008 £'000	1 October 2007 £'000
Amounts falling due within one year		
Balances with other central Government bodies		
Amount due from MoJ	3,655	1,681
Input VAT recoverable	34	56
Balances with bodies external to Government		
Prepayments	42	68
Staff debtors	60	39
Trade debtors	3,752	2,427
Accrued income	155	2,168
	7,698	6,439

Trade debtors are shown net of a provision for doubtful debts of £138,000

Amount due from MoJ represents funds owed by the Ministry of Justice.

10 CASH AT BANK AND IN HAND

Notes	31 March 2008 £'000
Balance at 1 October	405
Net cash inflow	158
Balance at 31 March	563
Of this amount the following balances at 31 March are held at:	
Office of HM Paymaster General	563

11 CREDITORS

	31 March 2008 £'000	1 October 2007 £'000
Amounts falling due within one year		
Accruals	696	575
Trade creditors	373	158
Deferred income	49	49
Tangible fixed asset creditors	290	535
	1,408	1,317
Amounts falling due after more than one year		
Deferred income	36	60
	1,444	1,377

Deferred income relates to the capital contributions received from the sub-under lessee (CAFCASS) towards its share of the leasehold improvements. This is being released to the Income and Expenditure account over the agency's lease term (see note 2.2).

12 PROVISIONS FOR LIABILITIES AND CHARGES

	Early departure costs £'000	Other £'000	Total £'000
Balance at 1 October 2007	137	936	1,073
Provided in the period	–	10	10
Provisions not required written back	–	–	–
Provisions utilised in the period	(25)	–	(25)
Balance at 31 March 2008	112	946	1,058

Early departure costs

The agency meets the additional costs of benefits beyond the normal PCSPS benefits in respect of employees who retire early by paying the required amounts annually to the PCSPS over the period between early departure and normal retirement date. The agency provides for this in full when the early retirement programme becomes binding on the agency by establishing a provision for estimated payments discounted by the real rate set by HM Treasury (currently 2.2 per cent).

Other

The above provision represents potential liabilities that the agency, in accordance with FRS 12, considers should be recognised at the balance sheet date, which includes financial losses (see Statement on Internal Control).

13 RECONCILIATION OF DEFICIT FOR THE YEAR TO CHANGES IN THE GENERAL FUND

	Notes	6 month period 2007/08 £'000
Deficit for the year		(2,392)
Notional charges		
Cost of capital charge	5	123
External auditor's remuneration	5	45
MoJ headquarters' support charges		
E-delivery group	5	1,300
Facilities management group	5	382
Human resources division	5	182
Other	5	312
MoJ funding		933
Transfer to general fund of realised element of revaluation reserve	14	44
Net increase in general fund		929
General fund at 1 October		9,436
General fund at 31 March		10,365

14 REVALUATION RESERVE

	Notes	31 March 2008 £'000
Balance at 1 October		172
Arising on revaluation during the year	8	344
Backlog depreciation	8	(132)
Transfer to general fund of realised element of revaluation reserve	13	(44)
Balance at 31 March		340

The revaluation reserve reflects the unrealised element of the cumulative balance of indexation and revaluation adjustments.

15 RECONCILIATION OF DEFICIT FOR THE YEAR TO NET CASH OUTFLOW FROM OPERATING ACTIVITIES

	Notes	6 month period 2007/08 £'000
Deficit for the year		(2,392)
Adjustments for notional and other non-cash charges:		
Deferred income	2.2	(24)
Cost of capital charge	5	123
MoJ headquarters' support charges		
E-delivery group	5	1,300
Facilities management group	5	382
Human resources division	5	182
Other	5	312
Depreciation	5	795
Loss on disposal	5	1
External auditor's remuneration	5	45
Provision for liabilities:		
Provided in the year	5	10
Adjustments for movements in working capital other than cash:		
(Increase)/decrease in debtors	9	(1,259)
(Decrease)/increase in creditors falling due within one year	11	336
Use of provisions	12	(25)
Net cash (outflow) inflow from operating activities		(214)

16 CAPITAL COMMITMENTS

Capital commitments at 31 March 2008 for which no provision has been made were £500,000.

17 COMMITMENTS UNDER OPERATING LEASES

Commitments under operating leases to pay future rentals during the financial year following the year of these accounts are given in the table below, analysed according to the period in which the lease expires:

	31 March 2008 land & buildings £'000
Expiry within one year	913
Expiry within two to five years	–
Expiry thereafter	–
Total	913

18 OTHER FINANCIAL COMMITMENTS

The OPG is a party to one Private Finance Initiative-type arrangement through its parent, the MoJ.

The cost of this contract is included within the OPG's MoJ headquarters' support charges as detailed in note 5. Under these arrangements the OPG does not incur any individual, third party operating, or capital commitments. The arrangement is the ARAMIS managed services agreement with Liberata UK Limited.

19 CONTINGENT LIABILITIES

The agency does not recognise any further liabilities over and above those provided for in the accounts, (see note 12); however, there remains a risk that further liabilities may be identified.

20 RELATED PARTY TRANSACTIONS

The agency is an executive agency of the MoJ. The Department is regarded as a related party. During the period the agency had various material transactions with the Department. In particular the agency's payroll cash flow (and accounting for advances and recoveries of salaries) was managed by the Department. In addition, the Department also provides internal audit services to the agency.

The agency works for the Court of Protection by implementing its orders and decisions. The Court is regarded as a related party. The Court's budget is also managed by the Chief Executive of the agency, after consultation with the Master of the Court of Protection.

The agency funds the Public Guardian Board (PGB), which has seven members independent of the OPG. There is no significant influence relating to financial or operating decisions. Costs are recorded in the financial statements and are included in the Remuneration Report where appropriate.

The agency also had transactions with other Government departments and entities. Most of these transactions have been with CAFCASS, which is the sub-under lessee of the agency's rented accommodation at Archway Tower. Income received from CAFCASS in the period amounted to £209,000.

None of the members of the Board of the agency, key managerial staff or other related parties has undertaken any material transactions with the agency during the financial year.

21 POST-BALANCE SHEET EVENTS

In accordance with the requirements of FRS 21, post-balance sheet events are considered up to the date on which the accounts are authorised for issue. This is interpreted as the date of the Certificate and Report of the Comptroller and Auditor General.

On 13 June 2008 it was announced that Martin John would take on the post of Public Guardian and Chief Executive of the OPG, with effect from 10 July 2008, following the departure of Richard Brook.

22 FINANCIAL INSTRUMENTS

FRS 13, Derivatives and Other Financial Instruments, requires disclosure of the role that financial instruments have had during the financial year in creating or changing the risks an entity faces in undertaking its activities. Because of the largely non-trading nature of its activities and the way in which government departments are financed, the agency is not exposed to the degree of financial risk faced by business entities.

Moreover, financial instruments play a much more limited role in creating or changing risk than would be typical of the listed companies to which FRS 13 mainly applies. The agency has very limited powers to borrow or invest surplus funds. Financial assets and liabilities are generated by day-to-day operational activities and are not held to change the risks facing the agency in undertaking its activities.

As permitted by FRS 13, debtors and creditors that mature or become payable within 12 months from the balance sheet date have been omitted from the currency profile.

Liquidity risk

The agency's net revenue resource requirement is financed by resources voted annually by Parliament to the MoJ, just as its capital expenditure largely is. It is not therefore exposed to significant liquidity risks. However, within the normal Parliamentary Supply procedure, the agency has to budget for resources (both revenue and capital) in the nine-month period preceding the financial year in which it will be granted.

Interest-rate risk

100 per cent of the agency's financial assets and 100 per cent of its financial liabilities carry nil or fixed rates of interest, and it is not therefore exposed to significant interest rate risk.

Foreign currency risk

The agency's exposure to foreign currency risk is not significant.

23 ACCOUNTABILITY

Fees remitted

There were 3,026 cases where fees were remitted. The total value was £387,000.

Cash losses

There were seven cases involving cash losses totalling £3,000.

Special payments

There were 85 special payments totalling £16,000.

Payments exceeding £250,000

There were no payments exceeding £250,000.

Measuring our
performance

KPI 1: Powers of Attorney

Enduring Powers of Attorney (EPAs) have been replaced by Lasting Powers of Attorney (LPAs). While EPAs may still be registered at any point in the future, they can no longer be made. LPAs are registered at the time of application and are not valid for use until registration is complete, subject to a 42-day statutory waiting period.

KPI purpose	Calculation method	Data source	Target 07/08	Achieved to 31 March 2008
To register an Enduring or Lasting Power of Attorney to enable use, where the OPG is satisfied that all is in proper order, as early as possible after the expiry of the statutory period for formal objections.	Percentage performance against target met is calculated by dividing the number of EPAs and LPAs registered within a specific period by total number of applications due to be registered and multiplying the quotient by 100.	Internal Organisation Data sourced from Stats worksheets held on 'P' drive and KPI CODES MS Access Database.	Register and return 98 per cent of correctly lodged LPAs/EPAs, where there are no objections, within five working days of the end of the statutory waiting period.	100% for EPAs 51% for LPAs
To inform an applicant of details of errors in applications as early as possible.	Percentage performance against target met is calculated by dividing the number of improperly made applications responded to within a specific period by the total number of improperly made applications identified and multiplying the quotient by 100.	Internal Organisation Data sourced from Stats worksheets held on 'P' drive and KPI CODES MS Access Database.	Inform the applicant where an application has not been made properly with details of the error within five working days of receipt in 80 per cent of cases.	3.6%

KPI 2: Supervision

All deputyship cases will require a supervision regime based on a risk assessment. Risk criteria include: whether a deputy has been refused credit or is an un-discharged bankrupt; whether the deputy has any financial interests which conflict with those of the client; the value of the client's estate; the relationship of the deputy to the client and any objections that were made to the appointment of the deputy.

KPI purpose	Calculation method	Data source	Target 07/08	Achieved to 31 March 2008
To ensure appropriate, effective and prompt monitoring of a deputy's actions. To ensure deputies are informed of their responsibilities within a specified timescale, and to make sure clients' interests are being protected as soon as possible.	Percentage performance calculated against target by dividing number of cases where supervision level set within period divided by number due and multiplying the quotient by 100.	Case data held on internal data management system – 'CASREC'.	90 per cent of deputyship cases will be assessed and a supervision level set within 30 days of the Court order being served on the Public Guardian.	99.4%
To review the effectiveness of the deputyship and ensure resource continues to be directed appropriately. To facilitate a regular review of any case-management issues.	Percentage performance calculated against target by dividing number of cases where supervision level reviewed within period divided by number due and multiplying the quotient by 100.	Case data held on internal data management system – 'CASREC'.	100 per cent of ongoing deputyships with active supervision will be reviewed within 13 months of the court order being issued.	None (But 100% scheduled within 13 months of court order)
To 'spot check' lighter touch cases and ensure no potential issues go unnoticed. To provide a deterrent against financial abuse. To recommend any changes that may be required to the Court of Protection.	Percentage performance calculated against target by dividing number of Type II cases audited within period divided by total number of Type II cases and multiplying the quotient by 100.	Case data held on internal data management system – 'CASREC'.	Audit 10 per cent of Type II supervision cases per year.	9% (in six months)

KPI 3: **Customer contact centre**

The contact centre will act as a point of communication for anybody contacting the OPG for advice and information about the OPG, the Court of Protection and other Mental Capacity Act (MCA)-related issues. It will also act as the first point of contact for most deputies in relation to queries about their powers and duties.

KPI purpose	Calculation method	Data source	Target 07/08	Achieved to 31 March 2008
To ensure customers are satisfied with the services they are accessing and to meet our standards of service delivery.	Percentage performance calculated against target by dividing number of items dealt with within a specified period divided by total number of items due to be dealt with and multiplying the quotient by 100.	Internal organisation data sourced from Stats worksheets held on 'P' drive and KPI CODES ACCESS Database.	Respond to 95 per cent of correspondence (including letters, faxes and emails) within 15 working days of receipt.	61.7%
To ensure all customers are able to access advice and OPG services within a reasonable timeframe.	Percentage performance calculated against target by dividing number of calls answered within target within a specified period divided by total number of calls received and multiplying the quotient by 100.	Internal organisation data sourced from telephone system.	85 per cent of telephone calls to the customer contact centre will be answered within 60 seconds.	76.1%
To ensure the performance measures for this new service are relevant and sufficiently robust.	Percentage performance calculated against target by dividing number of type II cases audited within period divided by total number of type II cases and multiplying the quotient by 100.	Case data held on internal data management system – 'CASREC'.	Monitor the use of the Customer Contact Centre and develop any further appropriate performance measures for 2008/09.	Performance measures for 2008/09 agreed

KPI 4: **Investigations**

We will carry out investigations where required.

KPI purpose	Calculation method	Data source	Target 07/08	Achieved to 31 March 2008
To ensure we act swiftly and appropriately whenever concerns about a client's welfare are raised.	Percentage performance calculated against target by dividing number of action plans put in place within a specified period by total number of action plans due and multiplying the quotient by 100.	Internal organisation data sourced from CASREC/ACCESS Reporting System.	Put in place an approved action plan in 100 per cent of investigations cases within 14 days of receipt.	100%
To ensure investigations are initiated and resolved, and that the Court of Protection is informed of any recommended changes at the earliest possible juncture.	Percentage performance calculated against target by dividing number of investigations completed within three months within a specified period by total number of investigations and multiplying the quotient by 100.	Internal organisation data sourced from CASREC/ACCESS Reporting System.	75 per cent of investigations will be completed within three months.	91.7%

KPI 5: **Customer satisfaction**

Based on inherited experience we will investigate, develop and agree a baseline for future customer satisfaction. We will carry out at least one customer satisfaction survey in the period to April 2008.

KPI purpose	Calculation method	Data source	Target 07/08	Achieved to 31 March 2008
To ensure customers are satisfied with the services available to them and with the standard of service delivery. To provide customer feedback to inform strategy. To enable monitoring of the organisation's management of customer expectation, and ensure all groups are represented.	–	–	Set an agreed process for surveying customer satisfaction.	Process agreed and survey conducted

KPI 6: **Cost recovery**

Based on the statutory instrument for fees approved by Parliament, we will aim to achieve the following targets for full cost recovery.

KPI Purpose	Calculation Method	Data Source	Target 07/08	Achieved to 31st March 2008
To ensure we work towards recovering the full costs of the OPG's services.	The cost recovery outturn is calculated using a full cost model to compare the income and expenditure streams of the OPG and Court of Protection. The cost estimates used in the model are based upon the full year forecast outturn for the OPG and the Court of Protection as taken from the Management Accounts each period. This represents the full resource-based cost of the organisation, including non-cash items and HQ recharges.	Full forecast outturn from monthly Management Accounts. Staff Numbers from the monthly staffing Returns from Heads of Division HQ Recharges.	100 per cent full cost recovery.	100%
To ensure we work towards recovering the full costs of the Court of Protection's services.	As above	As above	63 per cent full cost recovery.	63%

Our commitments
to you

1 We will reply to letters faxes and emails within 15 working days.
The standard was to respond to 95 per cent within 15 working days.
Overall performance for October to March was 61.7 per cent.

2 We will see visitors to our office within 10 minutes, with or without an appointment.
For visitors to named members of staff with no appointment: Between October and March, 43.2 per cent were seen within 10 minutes and 83.8 per cent were seen within 20 minutes.

3 We will aim to answer telephone calls within 60 seconds.
The standard was to answer 85 per cent within 60 seconds.
Overall performance for October to March was 76.1 per cent

4 If you request application forms or printed advice, we will post them within one working day.
Statistics for this are not currently available.

5 If you make a complaint, we will acknowledge it within two working days. Within 15 working days we will either provide a full response or explain why we cannot give a full response and when we will be able to do so.
Of complaints received between October and March, we acknowledged 94.2 per cent within five days and 95.3 per cent received a full reply within 15 days.

6 We will register an LPA or EPA within five working days of the end of the relevant waiting period – provided there are no issues or objections in relation to the application.
We have a target of 98 per cent. We achieved

100 per cent for EPAs and 51 per cent for LPAs.

7 We will inform the applicant for registration of an LPA or EPA if there are any errors in their application within 10 working days of receipt.
We have a target of 80 per cent in five days. We achieved 3.6 per cent in 10 days.

8 We will inform you of the type of supervision that applies to your deputyship and explain what this means within 35 working days of the OPG receiving the order from the Court.
We have a target of 90 per cent assessed within 30 days. We have achieved 99.4 per cent against this target.

9 We will contact the applicant within 25 working days of receipt of the formal application to the Court of Protection.
Against a target of 95 per cent in 20 working days we achieved 82.9 per cent. We achieved 87.32 per cent within 25 days.

10 Where no oral hearing is directed, the Court will give a direction within 21 weeks of receipt of the application.
Against a target of 75 per cent within 16 weeks we achieved 80 per cent. Against a target of 98 per cent in 20 weeks we achieved 87.5 per cent, reaching 92.1 per cent within 25 weeks.

11 Where an oral hearing is directed by the Court, we will set the hearing within 15 weeks of the direction.
Against a target of 75 per cent within six weeks we achieved 66.7 per cent. Against a target of 100 per cent within 14 weeks we achieved 94.1 per cent, reaching 95.8 per cent within 15 weeks.

Service Standards are the commitments we make to the people who use our services and these notes detail how we delivered on these commitments in the OPG's first six months.

Glossary

A

Attorney Person appointed by the donor to manage their financial and/or health and welfare affairs.

C

Case The name used to describe proceedings, whether to appoint a deputy, register an Enduring or Lasting Power of Attorney or any other legal remedy, instituted by someone seeking the Court of Protection to exercise its jurisdiction under the Mental Capacity Act.

Client A person whose affairs are the subject of the proceedings before the Court of Protection.

Court of Protection A superior court of record, whose function it is to protect the administration of property and health and welfare affairs of persons who, by reason of mental disorder, are incapable of managing their own affairs.

D

Donor The person who makes the Enduring or Lasting Power of Attorney, assigning responsibility for their financial and/or health and welfare affairs to an attorney.

Deputy The person appointed by the Court of Protection to manage the financial and/or health and welfare affairs of someone who is mentally incapacitated.

Deputyship An appointment by the Court of Protection that authorises a person (the deputy) to manage the financial and/or health and welfare affairs of a person who is, on medical evidence, incapable of doing so for themselves.

E

Enduring Power of Attorney (EPA) Document whereby a donor appoints an attorney to manage his or her financial affairs. (Note: EPAs have now been replaced by Lasting Powers of Attorney. It is no longer possible to make a new EPA, but they may still be registered.)

Executive agency Part of a Government department set up as a discrete operational unit to concentrate on providing a service to members of the public.

F

Fees Amounts charged to clients for services provided by the Office of the Public Guardian and Court of Protection.

I

Independent Mental Capacity Advocate (IMCA) A person appointed to represent the interests of an individual who lacks mental capacity when there is no other friend or family member available to support them.

K

Key Performance Indicator (KPI) A measure of the OPG's performance in key areas of its business.

L

Lasting Power of Attorney (LPA) Replaces Enduring Power of Attorney and includes provision for a donor to appoint someone to make decisions on their behalf in relation to finance and property and/or health and welfare matters, should they lose the mental capacity to do so.

M

Mental Capacity Act 2005 (MCA) Implemented on 1 October 2007, the Act makes new provisions for the protection of people who lack capacity to make their own decisions. It provides clear guidelines for people who make decisions on the behalf of others, and emphasises the rights of people to make their own decisions for as long as they are capable of doing so.

Ministry of Justice (MoJ) Formed on 9 May 2007, the Ministry of Justice combines the functions of the Department for Constitutional Affairs (including Her Majesty's Courts Service, the Tribunals Service and the Public Guardianship Office – now the Office of the Public Guardian) with those of the National Offender Management Service (including Her Majesty's Prison Service and National Probation Service). The MoJ also hosts the tri-lateral Office for Criminal Justice Reform.

O

Office of the Public Guardian (OPG) Replaces the Public Guardianship Office and is an executive agency of the Ministry of Justice, responsible for the administration and supervision of Enduring or Lasting Powers of Attorney and court-appointed deputyships.

P

Panel deputy A person who has demonstrated they have the skills and experience to act as a deputy in cases where there is nobody willing and suitable to do so.

V

Visit A visit to the client made by a court-appointed visitor to ensure their needs are being adequately met by their deputy.

Visitor An experienced person, often with a health or social care background, responsible for visiting clients on the instruction of the Court of Protection or the OPG.

"The Public Guardian Board will keep a close eye on the OPG in the following months to ensure the people who need our services are being properly protected"

ROSIE VARLEY OBE,
CHAIR OF THE PUBLIC
GUARDIAN BOARD

Printed in the UK for The Stationery Office Limited
on behalf of the Controller of Her Majesty's Stationery Office
ID 5849753 07/08

Printed on Paper containing 75% recycled fibre content minimum.